D1548239

# The
# *Hattie's*
## RESTAURANT
## COOKBOOK

# The
# *Hattie's*
# RESTAURANT
# COOKBOOK

*Classic Southern*
AND
*Louisiana Recipes*

## JASPER ALEXANDER

*Photography by Heather Bohm-Tallman*

**The Countryman Press**
A division of W. W. Norton & Company
*Independent Publishers Since 1923*

For information about permission to reproduce selections from this book, write to Permissions,
The Countryman Press, 500 Fifth Avenue, New York, NY 10110

For information about special discounts for bulk purchases, please contact
W. W. Norton Special Sales at specialsales@wwnorton.com or 800-233-4830

Library of Congress Cataloging-in-Publication Data

Names: Alexander, Jasper, author. | Bohm-Tallman, Heather, photographer.
Title: The Hattie's Restaurant Cookbook : Classic Southern and Louisiana
 Recipes / Jasper Alexander ; photography by Heather Bohm-Tallman.
Description: Woodstock, VT : Countryman Press, [2016] | Includes
bibliographical references and index.
Identifiers: LCCN 2016013900 | ISBN 9781581573466 (hardcover)
Subjects: LCSH: Cooking, American—Southern style. | Cooking,
American—Louisiana style. | Cooking—New York (State)—Saratoga Springs.
| Hattie's Restaurant (Saratoga, N.Y.) | LCGFT: Cookbooks.
Classification: LCC TX715.2.S68 A38 2016 | DDC 641.5975—dc23
LC record available at https://lccn.loc.gov/2016013900

The Countryman Press
www.countrymanpress.com
A division of W. W. Norton & Company, Inc.

500 Fifth Avenue, New York, NY 10110
www.wwnorton.com

10 9 8 7 6 5 4 3 2 1

This book is dedicated to

Hattie Moseley Austin.

# contents

**Introduction** 11

**How to Use this Book** 25

**Starters, Nibbles, and Noshes** 29

Spicy Pecans 31

Hushpuppies with Honey Butter 32

Caramelized Onion and Bacon Tart 35

Andouille Pigs in a Blanket 39

Cheese Straws and Olive Poppers 40

Good and Evil Chicken Wings 43

Fried Green Tomatoes with Buttermilk Dressing 47

Savory BBQ Shrimp 49

Crab Cakes with Sweet Corn Relish and Lime Mayo 51

Deviled Eggs 55

Andouille and Cheddar-Stuffed Mushrooms 57

Chicken Livers with Caramelized Onions and Bacon 59

Pimento Cheese 62

**Soups, Stews, and Food Served in a Bowl** 65

Brisket Chili 67

Steamed Clams with Saffron, Tomato, and Thyme 69

Macaroni and Cheese 71

Red Beans and Rice 75

Chicken and Dumplings 76

Crawfish Étouffée 79

Jambalaya 81

Gazpacho 84

Stone Soup 87

Shrimp, Andouille, and Corn Gumbo 88

**Oceans, Rivers, and Ponds** 91

Fried Catfish with Tartar Sauce Two Ways 93

Pecan-Crusted Trout with Tomato Bacon Jam 95

Crawfish Boil 99

Seared Sea Scallops with Grits, Watercress, and Brown Butter Balsamic Vinaigrette 102

Fried Oysters with Napa Cabbage Slaw and Cilantro Chutney 107

Salmon with Savoy Cabbage, Caramelized Pearl Onions, and Bacon 109

Panfried Softshell Crab over Cajun Coleslaw with Brown Butter Lemon Vinaigrette 111

Prosciutto-Wrapped Cod with Vegetables Provençal 114

Halibut with Wilted Spinach, Roasted Shiitakes, and Mushroom Nage 116

Frogs' Legs Sauce Piquant 120

Peel-and-Eat Shrimp 123

Monkfish with Clams and Chorizo 125

**Earth and Air** 129

Grilled Maple-Cured Pork Tenderloin 130

Pot Roast 132

Andouille and Pimento Cheese Sliders 136

Blackened Skirt Steak with Crispy Blue Cheese Grit Cakes and Smoked Tomato Butter 138

Warm Chicken, Bacon, and Arugula Salad 143

Chicken-Fried Steak 144

Ribs Without a Smoker 147

Hattie's Meat Loaf 150

Jerk Chicken with Tropical Fruit Salsa and Scallion Aioli 152

The Fried Chicken 155

## Side Dishes–Hot and Cold 159

Creamy Hominy 160

Smashed Potatoes 162

Creole Baked Beans 165

Biscuits 168

Corn and Tasso Spoon Bread 171

Basic Grits 173

Cajun Coleslaw 175

Corn Bread 177

Cranberry Coleslaw 178

Dirty Rice 180

Collard Greens 182

Salad Dressing (and Mason Jar Salad) 184

Candied Sweet Potatoes 187

Cucumber Salad 189

Savory Corn Bread Pudding 190

Hoppin' John Salad 192

## Breakfast and Brunch 195

The World's Best Egg Sandwich 196

Beignets 199

Two-Potato Ham Hash 202

Andouille, Caramelized Onion, and Cheddar Omelet 204

Biscuits and Sausage Gravy 206

Buttermilk Pancakes and Waffles 208

Pain Perdu 210

## Final Temptations 213

Sweet Potato Pie 214

Pecan Bread Pudding 216

Warm Chocolate Marquise 218

Pecan Pie 221

Key Lime Pie 222

Apple Crisp 226

Peach and Blueberry Cobbler 228


**Hattie's Cocktails** 231

Man-Hattie's 233

Firewater Punch 234

Classic Daiquiri 235

Hattie's Sangria 236

French Quarter Dark and Stormy 237

Mint Julep 238

Hattie's Mojito 239

Back Porch Lemonade 240

Cool as a Cucumber 241

Bloody Mary 242

Hot Toddy 243

Hard Sweet Tea 244

Sazerac 245

Pain Killer 246


**Basics and Fundamentals** 247


**Sources** 263


**Acknowledgments** 265


**Index** 267

Photo by Michael L. Noonan

# Introduction

"You want to do what?" This was my reaction when my wife first proposed that we move to the East Coast and buy Hattie's Chicken Shack. I thought she was delusional. We were both in the middle of successful careers in Seattle. We had just bought a house. We had an infant daughter. By all accounts, things were going as planned.

I was the chef of a well-respected Seattle restaurant and beginning to make a name for myself. She was booking private events for a swanky steakhouse and making great money. The Seattle food scene during the late nineties was exploding.

I had trained at the Culinary Institute of America, the most prestigious culinary school in the country. For four years after graduation, I'd cooked in some of the finest kitchens in New York, working alongside some of the best chefs around, culinary titans. I had James Beard awards to win, an empire to build. How were any of these things going to be accomplished frying chicken in Saratoga Springs?

Besides, I was a West Coast kid. Both my immediate and extended family had Southern roots, but my parents had left Washington, D.C., my birthplace, before my fifth birthday and I'd grown up in San Diego and Seattle.

I wasn't guilty of having a big-town prejudice. Actually I like small towns. I chose to go to college in Walla Walla, Washington, a town of about 30,000. And I had spent time in Saratoga and loved it. Six years earlier, I had met Beth there. In the spring of 1995, a fellow cook at Gramercy Tavern suggested I join him in spending the summer in Saratoga, working at Siro's. We were both transitioning from New York back to the West Coast. He was headed to San Francisco and I was going to try my hand at being a ski bum in Sun Valley, Idaho, for the winter and then plan my next serious career move. "What's Siro's?" I asked. "Summer camp for cooks—lots of booze and women and they pay a thousand bucks a week." Compared to stewing in the hot basement kitchens of New York for the summer, Saratoga sounded like heaven. So, I signed up, and Saratoga and Siro's delivered as billed.

I had a great time that summer, lounging and chasing bikinis at historic Victoria Pool during the day and cooking great food at night in a restaurant that was far better than I expected. Siro's was, at the time, a high-end seasonal restaurant that catered to those who fly themselves and their horses to Saratoga for the six-week meet at the Saratoga Race Course.

The most significant event of my summer was meeting Beth. She was a former professional ballet dancer who taught dance at a local arts school. As a native of the Saratoga area, she had worked at various local restaurants during summer breaks. That summer she was working at Siro's.

In the fall, she went back to teaching and I went to Sun Valley as planned, but soon we were coordinating cross-country trips. It was during one of these trips that I was introduced to Hattie's.

Beth was working there part time and sometimes I tagged along. Hattie's was far from what I was used to, but it was obviously a special place. The room was dripping with atmosphere. Not atmosphere manufactured by a restaurant designer, but the kind you find only in restaurants that have been around a long time—restaurants that have cultural and historical significance. Passing through the front door at Hattie's, it was easy to imagine being in a different time, surrounded by the collective memories of what had transpired there.

So, when Hattie's was quietly put on the market in 1999, Beth and I began considering what Hattie's already was and what it could be. We could freshen the menu, update the kitchen, really concentrate on the quality of what came out of it, and build on Hattie's historical presence in Saratoga. We could introduce a lively catering component that would serve innovative high-end food with a Southern or Cajun influence. We could strengthen the restaurant's ties to the community by sponsoring fund-raisers for local nonprofits, tying into its Southern theme.

That is what we have done in the 15 years we have owned Hattie's. This book chronicles our path: what we inherited from Hattie's iconic position in Saratoga and what we have created. The most tangible evidence of our business direction has been the opening of two new venues, the Track Shack, a seasonal concession at the Saratoga Race Course, and Hattie's Chicken Shack, a year-round quick-service restaurant that is conceptually centered on our core menu.

We have respected the legacy of Hattie Moseley Austin's generosity and nurturing spirit by staying actively engaged in community affairs and local philanthropic projects.

A major component of our community support is an annual Hattie's Mardi Gras fund-raiser. Since 2001, we have raised more than $650,000 for selected charities based in Saratoga Springs. We've also both served on the boards of a number of local nonprofit organizations related to the business community and local cultural and arts organizations. Our participation in local affairs keeps Hattie's tied to its founder's principles and to its mission as an institution.

# Hattie's Story

Hattie's is a restaurant that has been serving Southern cuisine for 78 years in a decidedly northern location. It reflects the history of its community, beginning with the glittering spa and gambling scene that brought Hattie Moseley Austin to Saratoga.

Accounts differ on some of the details and dates of Hattie Moseley Austin's history, but there's general agreement on the central story line. She was born Hattie Gray and was a native of Louisiana. She worked in the 1930s as a domestic cook for the A. E. Staleys, a Midwestern family that had made a fortune from processing cornstarch into household products. Hattie followed them regularly for many years from Chicago to Miami to Saratoga Springs, with occasional seasonal cooking at a few of Saratoga's hotels. Then, in 1938, she decided to stay in Saratoga and open her own restaurant, Hattie's Chicken Shack, which has evolved from a tiny store-front venture into an iconic, if unlikely, symbol of the community.

## *Hattie's on Federal Street*

The original Federal Street site of Hattie's Chicken Shack was on the west side of town, just around the corner from Saratoga's main commercial street, Broadway. In a 1985 interview, Hattie said, "I didn't have but $33. I bought a stove, an icebox, table, and chairs. It was very shoestring. It still is shoestring."

The West Side was a racially mixed neighborhood, mostly black, Italian, and Irish, and the restaurant's clientele was mixed, too. Congress Street, the center of Saratoga's blues and jazz clubs, was only a couple blocks from Hattie's and the chicken shack benefited from the proximity. For years Hattie's, stayed open 24 hours a day to accommodate the late-night crowd. Decades later Hattie was asked about good times at the Federal Street location. She recalled how everyone who'd been at Jack's Harlem Club until the wee hours would show up at her place for breakfast—famous people, show people, everybody.

Photograph courtesy of the George S. Bolster Collection of the Saratoga Springs History Museum

Hattie remembered one occasion when a big parade went by on South Federal. The crowd got louder, playing music and dancing and "just having a good time." A policeman asked her what was going on and she replied, "Honey, I don't know; all I know is I better go cook 'cause they're going to be awful hungry after this."

Charles Wait, chairman and CEO of the Adirondack Trust Bank, remembered the atmosphere at Hattie's: "Hattie's always represented a place where everybody in the community felt comfortable and it didn't matter if you were the president of the bank or a groom at the track. You would go there cheek to jowl, sit down and enjoy some good fried chicken and be treated the same, and everybody had a good time."

Dennis Mulholland, a Saratoga native who grew up on the West Side, often stopped at Hattie's for a bowl of grits or some biscuits on his way home from St. Peter's Academy. He was only ten or eleven, but "Hattie treated me just like she treated everybody else, like I was a regular, and in a way I was. Usually I paid for my food—grits and biscuits were cheap—but if Hattie had any day-old biscuits, she'd just give them to me and tell me to take them home to my mom."

When urban renewal came to Federal Street in the late 1960s, Hattie was forced to move the restaurant, and in 1970 she settled on the site of a defunct laundromat at 45 Phila Street that had originally been a lumber mill. Hattie's clientele followed, and though much remained the same, the larger space allowed her to expand the menu. Her husband, William Austin, skillfully ran the front of the house, graciously waiting tables, dressed in a tuxedo.

Much still remains the same. There have been kitchen equipment updates, new floors, cosmetic improvements to the dining area and patio, and a new HVAC system, but Hattie's has been in the same footprint for nearly 50 years.

**Hattie's Generosity.** When Hattie died in 1998, the recurring theme in her obituary was her generosity. From Ernie Waters, who worked for Hattie for thirty years: "[Hattie] treated me like a son." He recalled getting caught in a rainstorm and showing up in Hattie's kitchen, dripping. Hattie told him to take off his wet shirt and then handed him one of hers. City official Tom McTygue recalled, "Miss Hattie was the first person at the door after my father died." She brought a ham. When asked in 1985 how she liked being famous, Hattie was adamant: "Famous! I hate that word . . . my goal isn't to be famous—or to make a profit—my goal is to help whoever I can." And she did, from feeding anyone who was hungry to providing jobs to those who needed them most. Hattie never had any children of her own, but over the years we have had countless men and women come to us with stories about how Hattie treated them like a son or daughter. Hattie was also a trailblazer, though she might not have seen it that way. In her obituary, Charles Wait described her as "one of the first women libertarians. She didn't just talk about it, she did it."

# The MacLeans

Christel and Colin MacLean bought Hattie's from Hattie Austin in 1993. She was then in her late 80s and felt she could no longer deal with the long hours of cooking and hands-on operation of the restaurant. The MacLeans owned and managed the restaurant for eight years, honoring Hattie's legacy of good food at fair prices. They maintained the heritage of Southern and Louisiana cooking, but added some more contemporary dishes and acquired a liquor license, virtually a requirement in a resort town.

They added a festive tented area on the back patio of the restaurant to increase the bar space and accommodate the summer overflow crowds. They were effective ambassadors of the restaurant's image, including designing the stick figure chicken that became the restaurant's logo and promoting the restaurant in regional and national publications. They polished Hattie's image and reputation and brought the operation into the twenty-first century.

# 45 Phila Street

One of the costs of having a charming historical property like 45 Phila is sacrificing efficiency, and sometimes even potential profit, for atmosphere.

**The Dining Room.** The main dining room is a rectangle about 25 x 25 feet. Its maximum capacity is 45 people and it doesn't hurt if they are friendly. Until recently, a loud and cranky ceiling-mounted HVAC system competed with customers' conversations, and it was always either too hot or too cold. There's no real bar inside, just a service bar, allegedly salvaged from the demolition of a former grand hotel. Thankfully, for eight or nine months of the year, there's plenty of room for a long bar and 30 more customers at tables on the tented and heated patio. Recently we've entered into an agreement with the city that turned Lena Lane, the alley that runs alongside our building, into a pedestrian walkway and sidewalk café.

**The Kitchen.** To say that the kitchen at Hattie's is not ideal is a gross understatement. We make do with what we have, but we push the limits of what is possible. The kitchen is very small and has several bottlenecks that require one to be quite friendly and comfortable with one's coworkers. To compensate for lack of square footage, the kitchen is built like a submarine. There is not a square inch of unused space. In the busy summer months, we run two separate crews just so we'll have enough room to work safely and stay organized. The reality is it makes us better at our jobs. We are more efficient and more organized because we have to be. There are two things that make the space less confining than it might otherwise be: 14-foot ceilings and two large double-hung windows that face the alley. One of the windows is at the end of the cooking line, and for years, I've enjoyed being able to lean out and talk to customers and whoever might be passing by.

Photograph © 1979 by Mary Ann Lynch

**The Pit of Despair.** As much as we appreciate the natural light, we know a dark, damp underbelly lies beneath our feet. Officially Saratoga has 17 mineral springs, but we know of one more, and it's under Hattie's kitchen. In 2002 we had to replace the rickety kitchen floor. In the process, we found a hatch in the subfloor and a ladder of sorts leading down to a dirt-floor crawl space. We dug a pit, poured a concrete slab, replaced the electrical and plumbing, and installed a hot water heater in our "cellar," which freed up a few square feet of space in our kitchen. But then we had a torrential rain and our hot water heater died. Specifically it drowned. We limped along for about a year, descending into the Pit of Despair regularly to tinker with the unhappy appliance. Eventually we gave up. Between natural springs, torrential summer rainstorms, spring snow melt, and bedrock that refuses to drain, our cellar is useless. We have since mitigated the effects of our underground spring by installing a drain and pump system and hanging our hot water heater on the wall.

## *Café Lena*

We rent our charming but sometimes challenging space at 45 Phila from Café Lena, the oldest continuously running folk coffeehouse in North America. In the 1960s, the popularity of folk music spread from urban centers to less likely locales, such as Saratoga Springs. Lena Spencer, an actress, ran the café for 29 years. There was nothing elaborate about the physical space, but her musicians were remarkable. She selected her artists with a fine ear, nurtured them, and provided them with a place to sing their songs. Arlo Guthrie, Pete Seeger, Don McLean, and Bob Dylan are among the many alumni of the coffeehouse. When Lena died in 1989, a group of her supporters formed a nonprofit organization to continue her mission. This group was able to purchase 47 Phila and the adjoining building, 45 Phila, which we occupy. These two landmark historical businesses are bound by the same goals. We respect the character and accomplishments of the two remarkable women who shared this corner of Saratoga. We also know that, in order for their legacies to survive, we must stay current and accept the challenges of change. We fully support each other, grateful that we will have a shared future as well as a shared past.

## Stewardship and Evolution

From a chef's perspective, owning a historic restaurant that has been in business for 78 years can be limiting. I must always remember that the collective memory of my customers spans generations and that the continued success of the restaurant relies on ensuring consistent food memories for my customers. I hope I have managed to appreciate what I inherited and blend my own culinary sensibilities into a menu that continuously evolves but never loses sight of its past.

My formal training at the Culinary Institute of America and my New York and West Coast experiences have provided a solid foundation of culinary knowledge. As a chef, I build on this to learn, grow, and explore new ideas. Realistically, not all these ideas are going to be applicable to the menu at Hattie's. In many cases I have been able to use our catering company as an outlet to explore new ideas. Like most chefs, I also enjoy creating new dishes when I'm cooking at home for family and friends. The recipes in *The Hattie's Restaurant Cookbook* are drawn from all my resources. I think they provide a balanced approach to my take on classic Southern and Louisiana food.

## Getting It Done

My father was a newspaperman, not a restaurateur, and while the two industries share little in common, there is one significant similarity. Restaurants, like newspapers, must without fail produce a product on a daily basis, and because of that, you're only as good as your last day. To succeed, let alone thrive under this type of pressure requires consistent effort from a number of people who are aligned toward a common goal. Beth and I are very lucky to have enjoyed this type of environment at Hattie's during our tenure. Actually, the thing Beth and I are most proud of, and something that rarely makes the papers or the bottom of plaques, is the quality and stability of our staff. For many reasons, restaurants often have a revolving door of employees. This has never been the case at Hattie's. Currently, with many of our children at working age, we are

training the second generation of Hattie's employees. Some of our most valuable employees have been at the restaurant longer than we have.

Mike, who started at the restaurant the summer before we bought it, has been the most trusted and dependable kitchen employee I have ever had the privilege of working with. Other than perhaps Hattie, he has baked more biscuits and corn bread, fried more chicken, and pulled more pies out of the oven than anyone, including me. He is confident, focused, and unflappable regardless of the situation. While those qualities are important, it's Mike's ability to lead and deal with people that is his real skill. He is an astute judge of character and a natural leader, with no interest in the trappings that usually come with positions of influence. He is truly the glue that holds everything together.

Aime and her husband, Thom, have been loyal friends and supporters without peer since day one, and Aime's skill as a bookkeeper and money juggler, along with her general counsel, have been invaluable. Both Annette and Ernie preceded our arrival at Hattie's by years, and

have strengthened the thread that connects us to the restaurant's past. Llona, Maryann, and Jaime are the dynamic team behind Hattie's catering. They balance clients' desires with logistical constraints and ensure food integrity while executing the smoke-and-mirror magic of striking presentations. Hillary and Trunks also worked at Hattie's before we arrived, starting when they were both only 15. Trunks has literally worked every

position in the restaurant, and even though he is a full-time engineer by day, he still bartends on the weekends. Hillary moved from busser, to waiter, to manager, to operations director for the whole company. Her energy, attention to detail, and thoroughness have always played a significant role. Currently she has returned to manage the Chicken Shack and streamline processes for possible future expansion. Sal has been our bar manager for 13 years and he still won't tell us what's in the Bloody Mary mix. Despite his penchant for secrecy, which is not a bad trait in a bartender, he has been a loyal and scrupulously honest employee and a goodwill ambassador to our customers.

Fifteen years ago Beth and I bought a historic restaurant and committed ourselves and our family to the joys and frustrations of running a family business. There have been far more good times than bad, and although it has never been easy, it has always been rewarding. We joke about how she was supposed to be the face of the company, and I would work quietly in the background, where I was more comfortable and perfectly content. Then a few years into our tenure, the Food Network called and wanted us to be on the show *Throwdown with Bobby Flay*. We were and I won, and that changed our paradigm for good. The spotlight was now on me simply for doing what I did every day and for being in the right place at the right time.

Beth has been, and always will be, the driving force behind the success of Hattie's. Her energy is kinetic, and she often accomplishes more by 10 AM than I will in a whole day. She deftly juggles virtually all front-of-the-house matters, scheduling, hiring, firing, restaurant marketing, customer and staff correspondence, public and press relations, special events, social media, and all charitable endeavors, all while still being a physical presence in the restaurant and telling me when and where I'm supposed to be and what I should wear. Buying Hattie's was her idea in the first place, and even though I'm the one writing this book, I wouldn't be writing it without her. She is more than a partner in life and business; she is also my boss, and I mean that quite literally. She owns 51 percent of the company. So, the Tallent would like to thank you and remind you that you are the extra *l*.

# How to use This Book

Please read the introductions to the recipes. You'll find cooking tips, ingredient descriptions, explanations, possible substitutions, and suggested sources.

Please read the section "Notes on Frying at Home" (page 248) before you attempt deep-frying unless you're very familiar with the process. This section points out some messy and even dangerous pitfalls that can be easily avoided.

Read the entire recipe before you start. I've tried to avoid surprises at the end, but sometimes the last step isn't a quick step—such as a sauce needing to reduce for 20 minutes.

Don't be surprised to find recipes within recipes. In dishes that are composed of several parts, this layout seems preferable to scattering the various components of a recipe throughout the book. Following recipes that jump around requires a lot of bookmarks and a lot of patience.

## Ingredients

I always use Diamond kosher salt. Almost all restaurants use this salt, and it's worth seeking out. It's milder than both table salt and sea salt and has a more balanced flavor. If you must use other salts, especially iodized table salt, cut the amount the recipe calls for in half.

Pepper, black or white, is always freshly ground. I don't expect that you will grind the pepper into a bowl and then measure it out for a particular recipe. Use the measurements as a guide and grind fresh

to your own preferences. If you substitute finely ground commercial pepper for freshly ground, use half the amount called for in the recipe.

I have assumed that all andouille and chorizo sausage is fully cooked. If you should come across some that isn't, simmer it in a little water or brown it in the oven until it is fully cooked before using it in a recipe.

Flour is all-purpose unless otherwise specified in a recipe. Milk is always whole. Butter is always unsalted. Maple syrup is real and pure.

When a frozen vegetable is used as a substitute for fresh, it should be thawed unless it's being added to a liquid dish, such as gumbo.

# Equipment

As for pans, I don't have a long list of special equipment because it just isn't necessary, but a couple of things are particularly convenient to have. One is a cast-iron skillet, preferably about 12 inches in diameter. A sturdy nonstick skillet of about the same size can be useful for cooking fish. You'll need a heavy Dutch oven for a couple of dishes, and possibly for frying. It's good to have a substantial stockpot that holds around 8 quarts for making things served in bowls, such as chili or gumbo.

You don't need many pots and pans, and they don't have to cost a fortune or have a chef's name on the lid. They do have to have heavy bottoms and be made of high-quality materials. You are more likely to find good-quality pots and pans at an estate sale, where they have graced someone's kitchen for decades, than you are at a big-box store.

Strictly speaking, a blender or food processor is not a necessity, but it makes short work out of long and tedious work. I don't recommend them for chopping because they don't cut cleanly—they mush—but because of this, they are perfect for pulverizing food.

Stand mixers look great on your kitchen counter and are certainly a useful tool if you do a lot of baking, but a $10 hand mixer from the grocery store will work just fine in almost all applications. Keep in mind that any modern mechanical kitchen tool is really just a time saver. Any recipe or method in this book, or almost any cookbook for that matter, can be done by hand. People were cooking great food long before any of these tools were invented.

You will also find that an inexpensive instant-read thermometer and a candy thermometer will come in handy for checking meat temperatures and frying.

## Fundamentals

This book is not intended to be encyclopedic like *The Joy of Cooking*, which explains methods and variations in great detail. At the same time I don't want you to have to pick up another book or go online to find a basic recipe for something that is required for a particular dish. I have included a section at the end of the book with basic preparations for items that are repeated throughout the book.

# starters, Nibbles, and Noshes

# Spicy Pecans

Consider yourself warned: These little beauties are addictive. This recipe uses a potent blend of cayenne pepper, chili powder, and paprika mixed into a French meringue that, when baked, encases the pecans in a spicy, sweet shell. The result is crispy, sweet, and spicy pecans that are hard to stop eating once you start. Make a batch of these for your next party or just for the family for movie night or a ball game. They're always a hit. While we usually stick to pecans, the recipe will work with any nut or nut mixture you like.

1. Preheat oven to 350°F.

2. Beat the egg whites by hand with a whisk or an electric mixer in a nonreactive bowl until they are foamy and have doubled in volume.

3. Slowly add the sugar while whisking. Continue to whisk until the meringue thickens to form stiff peaks.

4. Fold in the salt, spices, Worcestershire, and hot sauce with a rubber spatula.

5. Fold in the pecans, coating them evenly. Turn out the pecans in a single layer onto a greased or nonstick baking pan.

6. Place the pan in the oven and bake for about 5 minutes. Pull out the pan and you will see that the meringue has puffed up. With a spoon or spatula, mix and move the nuts around, turning them over and breaking apart any large clumps. Return the pan to the oven for 10 to 15 minutes, mixing the nuts every now and again to make sure they cook evenly.

7. When the nuts are dry and toasted, remove from the oven and allow to cool before breaking up any clumps.

**Yield: 1 pound pecans**

3 large egg whites

½ cup sugar

1 teaspoon kosher salt

1 tablespoon cayenne pepper

1 tablespoon paprika

1 tablespoon chili powder

2 teaspoons Worcestershire sauce

2 teaspoon Hattie's Hot Sauce or Louisiana-style hot sauce

1 pound (4 to 5 cups) pecan halves

# Hushpuppies with Honey Butter

Hushpuppies are most often served as a side dish to fried fish, but at Hattie's we think ours are good enough to stand on their own, so we serve them as appetizers. A hushpuppy is essentially just a corn and onion fritter. Ours are just shy of a golf ball in size and are crunchy on the outside and full of onions and freshly shucked corn on the inside.

The origin and history of the hushpuppy is up for some debate, but as the story goes, Confederate soldiers would toss bits of fried cornmeal to their dogs to "hush the puppies" and not give away their position. We continue the tradition today and use them to appease patrons who are patiently waiting for their table.

The real trick to making good hushpuppies is the consistency of the finished batter. It should look like wet sand and be slightly sticky and elastic. You can make the batter a day or two in advance, but remember the cornmeal will absorb the liquid over time, so the batter may need to be adjusted with more buttermilk. Always cook a test hushpuppy to check the consistency and seasoning. It will look loose floating in the oil until it begins to brown, but it should not fall apart.

We serve Honey Butter as a spread for our hushpuppies and with biscuits and cornbread for brunch. It would be equally delicious on dinner rolls.

**Yield: 15 to 20 hushpuppies**

1 cup cornmeal

½ cup all-purpose flour

1 tablespoon baking powder

2 tablespoons sugar

1½ teaspoons kosher salt, plus more for sprinkling

½ teaspoon onion powder

¼ teaspoon freshly ground black pepper

½ cup grated onion, with the juice

½ cup corn kernels, fresh or frozen, thawed

1 large egg

½ cup buttermilk

3 cups vegetable oil or your preferred frying setup

1. Combine the cornmeal, flour, baking powder, sugar, salt, onion powder, and pepper in a medium bowl and blend with a whisk.

2. Add the grated onion, onion juice, and corn to the dry ingredients and mix with a spoon or rubber spatula until evenly distributed.

3. In a small bowl, whisk the egg and buttermilk together.

4. Add the buttermilk mixture to the dry ingredients and whisk together until it resembles wet sand.

5. Heat the oil in your preferred frying setup until a candy thermometer reads 350°F (see note).

*(Continued)*

6. Carefully ease a scoop of the batter into the hot oil. Scoop the batter with one spoon and then scrape the batter into the oil with the back of the second spoon. Release the batter close to the surface of the oil so you don't splash hot oil everywhere. Add more scoops of batter to the pan, but do not crowd; cook in batches if necessary.

7. The hushpuppies will initially sink to the bottom of the pan but once a crust begins to form on the bottom side, they should float up to the surface of the oil. If they are sticking to the bottom, gently release them with a slotted spoon.

8. Cook for about 5 minutes total. You will want to gently turn and move the hushpuppies around to ensure that they cook evenly. Keep an eye on your temperature, adjusting the heat to maintain 350°F.

9. Once the hushpuppies are golden brown, remove with a slotted spoon and place on a tray lined with paper towels. Season with a little sprinkling of salt. Like all things fried, hushpuppies are best eaten shortly after frying, but they can be held warm in a 200°F oven, if necessary.

**NOTE:** Because of the baking powder, the hushpuppies are going to want to float to the top shortly after you put them in the oil, assuming you have enough oil in the pan. For this reason, there is no real advantage to deep-frying over panfrying. The exception would be if you have a tabletop deep fryer. Choose a pan or pot big enough to fry five or six hushpuppies at a time and add just enough oil so that hushpuppies can float off the bottom, making them easier to handle. The amount of oil used will be more than would typically be used for panfrying, but far less than for deep-frying.

## Honey Butter

**Yield: ½ cup butter**

½ cup (1 stick) unsalted butter, at room temperature

2 tablespoons honey

1 teaspoon kosher salt

1. Blend the butter, honey, and salt together in a small bowl with a wooden spoon or rubber spatula.

2. Honey butter will keep for months, stored in an airtight container under refrigeration.

## Caramelized Onion and Bacon Tart

This recipe should be considered a jumping-off point for some spirited experimentation. I learned it from an Austrian pastry chef I worked with ages ago. The all-butter tart dough is rich, flaky, delicious, and virtually foolproof in its simplicity. It provides a perfect blank canvas for any type of sweet or savory application. This style of tart is great on its own as an appetizer or as a light lunch accompanied by a green salad. The caramelized onions provide a base, and you can vary the other ingredients depending on what you have, what you like, or what's in season. Wild mushrooms, grilled vegetables, asparagus, tomatoes, cheese, no cheese, almost anything you can think of will work. Choose high-quality smoky bacon for this variation; it's really the star of the show. I firmly believe that where bacon is concerned, you really can't have enough, so I call for a whole pound. If you are not quite as fervent about bacon as I am, you could back it off a bit.

*(Continued)*

## Tart dough:

2 cups all-purpose flour, plus
more for dusting

1 teaspoon kosher salt

1 teaspoon sugar

1 cup (2 sticks) unsalted butter,
chilled, cut into ½-inch pieces

½ cup ice water

## Filling:

2 tablespoons olive oil, plus more
if needed

1 pound sliced bacon

8 cups sliced onions

4 garlic cloves, finely chopped

2 teaspoons kosher salt

1 teaspoon freshly ground black
pepper

2 tablespoons chopped fresh
rosemary, divided

2 tablespoons chopped fresh
thyme, divided

2 tablespoons chopped fresh
parsley, divided

1. **Prepare the tart dough:** Combine the flour, salt, and sugar in a food processor and pulse a few times to combine.

2. Add the cold butter and pulse until the mixture looks like coarse cornmeal.

3. Slowly add the water until the mixture just starts to come together—if it sticks together when you squeeze it, as opposed to crumbling apart, you have added enough water. You might not need the entire ½ cup of water; you don't want to overmix the dough or have it be too wet, so less is more.

4. Turn out the dough onto a work surface and gather it together with your hand, pressing and flattening it until it is ¼ to ½ inch thick. Any shape you want is fine. It does not need to be a circle, but the dough should roughly resemble the shape of the final tart, which itself will be uneven.

5. Wrap the dough in plastic wrap and put it in the refrigerator for at least an hour while you prepare your filling.

1. **Prepare the filling:** Heat the olive oil in a large sauté pan over medium heat. Sauté the bacon for about 10 minutes or until the fat is rendered and the bacon is browned but not crisp. Remove the bacon from the pan with a slotted spoon and drain on a paper towel. The tart still has to bake, so if the bacon is crispy now, it might be too crisp after it comes out of the oven.

2. Add the onions and garlic to the bacon drippings. Season with salt and pepper and cook over medium heat, stirring frequently until the onions turn a deep golden brown. This could take as long as 30 minutes, depending on the heat and the sugar content of the onions. If they start to look dry, add a little more olive oil and adjust the heat if necessary.

3. Once the onions have caramelized, add half the chopped herbs and half the cooked bacon and mix thoroughly. Remove from the heat and allow to cool for a few minutes. You don't want the onion mixture cold, but you don't want to put hot onions on your buttery

tart dough, either. By the time you preheat the oven and roll out your pastry, they will be fine.

4. Preheat oven to 375°F.

5. **Assemble the tarts:** Roll out the dough on a lightly floured work surface until it's ⅛-inch thick. The exact shape does not really matter. This is intended to be a rustic-looking tart. Transfer the dough to a baking sheet.

6. Spread the onion mixture evenly over the dough, leaving a 1-inch border around the edge. Sprinkle the remaining bacon over the top and fold the border back over the onions. Remember, rustic tart, so if you're getting some pleats and folds in the dough, go with it; they will be pretty in the end.

7. Bake for 35 to 40 minutes or until the pastry is golden brown. Remove from the oven and sprinkle the remaining herbs over the top. Serve warm or at room temperature. If you're going to serve the tart as an appetizer, cut it into smaller pieces, about 1½-inch square. If you're going to serve it as a lunch or light supper, just cut it into quarters.

# Andouille Pigs in a Blanket

Nostalgia and memories of the cocktail weenie version are largely responsible for the popularity of this appetizer. The other part of the equation is that they are delicious to the point of being addictive. The simple twist of replacing the bland cocktail weenie with a great piece of andouille sausage and using rich puff pastry transforms the dish. They are super easy to make and are a great choice for any gathering. Puff pastry sheets are becoming more common in grocery stores and are usually located along with the phyllo dough in the freezer section. If your store does not carry puff pastry, try buying a sheet from your local bakery. If all else fails, unroll the crescent rolls you can buy in the cardboard tube, With some creative trimming, you can make it work.

**Yield: 20 to 25 pieces**

1 sheet puff pastry, about 13 x 18 inches

1 pound andouille sausage

1 large egg, beaten

1. Line a tray that will fit in your freezer with waxed paper.

2. Lay the puff pastry sheet on your work surface. The size of your sausage will dictate how you cut the dough, but the idea is to have the dough cover all but the very ends of the sausage. So, cut rectangles that are ¼ inch narrower than the sausage is wide (see note).

3. Place the sausage at one end of the dough and roll the dough around the sausage, leaving a ⅛- to ¼-inch margin of unwrapped dough.

4. Rub a little beaten egg on the unwrapped margin of dough, seal with your finger, and place on the lined tray. Continue until all the sausages are wrapped in puff pastry. Place the tray of sausages in the freezer for about 20 minutes to make them easier to cut.

5. While the sausages are chilling, preheat oven to 400°F.

6. Remove the sausages from the freezer and cut into rounds about ½-inch thick. Place cut side down about an inch apart on a baking sheet. Bake for about 20 minutes or until the pastry has puffed up and turned golden brown.

**NOTE:** Because of the butter content of the puff pastry, it goes from thawed and pliable to ultrasoft and unworkable fairly quickly, depending on the temperature. You can put the dough back in the refrigerator or freezer for a few minutes if it becomes uncooperative. Sprinkling a bit of cornmeal on your work surface will help keep the dough from sticking.

# Cheese Straws and Olive Poppers

In the South, it's virtually impossible to go a party and not find some cheese straws somewhere. Not the case up here in the great Northeast. I can safely say that in the 15 years I've been back in Saratoga, I have never even seen a cheese straw outside our own catering events or at Hattie's. I hate to say it, but most people up here don't know a cheese straw from a bread stick.

We have used them at the restaurant as bar snacks and they are also quite popular for caterings. We almost always have a few pounds of cheese straw dough in the freezer, so even if the client doesn't order cheese straws, if it's a Southern-themed party, I'll make them anyway. They have a distinct cheese flavor with just enough spice to keep you reaching for more, are consistently crisp, and are easy to make.

**Yield: about 75 cheese straws**

½ cup (1 stick) unsalted butter, at room temperature, cut into ½-inch pieces

1 pound grated extra-sharp cheddar cheese

1½ cups all-purpose flour, plus more for dusting

¼ teaspoon cayenne pepper

¼ teaspoon red pepper flakes

½ teaspoon kosher salt

1 tablespoon half-and-half

1. Preheat oven to 350°F and gather two large baking sheets.

2. In a stand mixer fitted with the paddle attachment, cream the butter until it is light yellow, 3 to 4 minutes. Add the cheese to the bowl and blend until well combined, about 30 seconds. If you don't have a stand mixer, don't worry. A hand mixer with a beater attachment will work. You can even cream the butter with the cheese by beating them together with the back of a wooden spoon. This will take a little longer, but the results will be fine.

3. Add the flour, cayenne, red pepper flakes, and salt and work into the dough with the back of a wooden spoon. Add the half-and-half and continue to work until everything is well combined and the mixture comes together to form a dough ball.

4. Turn out the dough onto a floured surface and press the dough into a nice uniform rectangle about ½-inch thick. With a lightly floured rolling pin, roll the dough down to ¼-inch in thickness (see note).

5. Cut the dough into individual strips about ¼-inch wide and transfer to your baking sheets, leaving about ¼-inch of space between each straw (see note).

*(Continued)*

6. Bake for 10 to 15 minutes or until golden brown. Remove from the oven and allow the baked straws to cool. If you're not going to serve them immediately, store them in an airtight container. The finished product will be quite delicate, so be careful when transferring and serving, so they don't break.

**NOTE:** Because of the ratio of cheese and butter to the amount of flour, this dough is very stiff when it is cold and very soft if it gets too warm. After you roll out the dough and before you cut it, transfer it to a cookie sheet, cover it with plastic wrap, and put it in the refrigerator for 30 minutes. The dough will stiffen up considerably and make cutting and placement of the individual straws much easier.

There is no rule to the length of the cut straws, so cut them to whatever length you wish. You can also use pastry or cookie cutters to make different shapes.

If the recipe makes more straws than you need, you can divide the unbaked dough into portions and freeze them for later use.

## Olive Poppers

As a variation, we also use this cheese straw dough for olive poppers. Here's how—short version. Pinch off a piece of dough and roll it into a ball a little bigger than an olive. While you hold it in the center of your palm, poke an indentation in the ball with your thumb, stick a medium-size pitted Kalamata or Spanish green olive in the hole, and smooth the dough around the olive. Repeat. It's faster than it sounds. Bake according to the directions above.

## Good and Evil Chicken Wings

Sometimes as chefs, and certainly as restaurant owners, we have no choice but to bend to the will of the people. There is no better example of this on the Hattie's menu than our chicken wings. When Beth and I bought the restaurant, it did not surprise me that Hattie's had chicken wings on the menu. After all, this bar food staple was invented a few hours down the road in Buffalo.

What did surprise me was the Asian-inspired preparation. The sauce was made with a mixture of hot sauce, oyster sauce, hoisin sauce, and butter. Not only did this not make sense conceptually for the restaurant, but also, if you're going for an Asian-style wing, where was the ginger and the garlic, a little soy or ponzu, some sesame oil or a dash of Asian fish sauce, and maybe some cilantro? So, I did what a good chef does: I fixed it. I had been the chef of one of the best Pacific Rim restaurants in Seattle. I could whip up an Asian-style wing sauce in my sleep.

*(Continued)*

Except there was a problem—no one liked my new wings. I thought they were better, more balanced, and certainly more authentic in their flavor profile than what we had been serving. But sometimes that's not the point. Making our customers happy is the point. You can fry these original recipe wings using any of the frying setups or, alternatively, bake them in the oven. We serve them with celery sticks and Pecan Blue Cheese Dressing (recipe follows).

## For fried wings:

**Yield: 2 dozen wings**

¼ cup vegetable oil if baking, or your preferred deep frying setup

12 whole chicken wings, cut in half, wing tips removed

¼ cup hoisin sauce

¼ cup oyster sauce

¾ cup Hattie's Hot Sauce or commercial Louisiana-style hot sauce

2 tablespoons unsalted butter

¼ cup chopped scallions

2 tablespoons chopped fresh parsley

1. Get your preferred fryer setup going and heat your oil to 325° to 350°F.

2. Dry the wings thoroughly with cloth or paper towels. Any water on the wings could make your fryer bubble, hiss, and potentially boil over.

3. Fry the wings for about 10 minutes or until they are browned, crispy, and fully cooked.

4. While the wings are frying, get your sauce ready: Warm the hoisin sauce, oyster sauce, hot sauce, and butter in a large sauté pan over low heat. The butter should melt and the sauce should be hot, but it should not simmer or reduce.

5. When the wings are fully cooked and crispy, transfer them to the sauté pan with a slotted spoon or spider and increase the heat to medium. Toss and shake the wings so they are evenly coated with the sauce. Add the scallions and parsley and toss a few more times.

6. Transfer into a bowl or onto a platter and serve with some celery sticks and Pecan Blue Cheese Dressing (recipe follows).

## For baked wings:

1. Preheat oven and a baking pan, preferably nonstick, to 400°F.

2. Rinse and drain the wings in a colander, spread them out on a baking sheet lined with a towel, and pat them dry.

3. In a large bowl, toss the wings with the oil and spread out evenly in a single layer on your preheated baking pan. Cook for about 20 minutes, then flip the wings over and cook for an additional 20 minutes so that both sides are browned and crispy. When the wings have about 5 minutes left, continue with steps 4 through 6 in the above method.

## Pecan Blue Cheese Dressing

**Yield: 1½ cups dressing**

1 cup crushed pecans

5 ounces blue cheese, crumbled

½ cup sour cream

¼ cup buttermilk

¼ cup mayonnaise

1 teaspoon freshly squeezed lemon juice

½ teaspoon Hattie's Hot Sauce or commercial Louisiana-style hot sauce

¼ teaspoon Worcestershire sauce

½ teaspoon kosher salt

½ teaspoon freshly ground black pepper

1. Preheat oven to 350°F and toast the crushed pecans for about 10 minutes or until they are browned and have a pleasant toasted nut aroma. Remove from the oven and allow to cool.

2. Whisk together the blue cheese, sour cream, buttermilk, mayonnaise, lemon juice, hot sauce, Worcestershire, salt, and pepper in medium bowl until well combined. Smash some of the larger blue cheese crumbles against the side of the bowl with a wooden spoon to thicken and enhance the body of the dressing. Add the cooled nuts. Store in an airtight container in the refrigerator for up to a week.

# Fried Green Tomatoes with Buttermilk Dressing

While there is little question that fried chicken is the most iconic of Southern specialties, fried green tomatoes have got to be near the top of the list. The question, however, is: Why? I believe it might have more to do with Fannie Flagg's book and the subsequent movie than any true regional origin. I canvassed my family, whom I often turn to for Southern reference, and no one has any childhood memories of eating fried green tomatoes. My first memory of eating green tomatoes was the pickled variety found on the tables of any self-respecting Jewish delicatessen. In the Northeast we have a relatively short growing season, so green tomatoes are plentiful, with a healthy surge in the fall when we run out of the warm summer sun necessary for ripening. Regardless of their heritage, the slightly acidic nature of a green tomato responds well to frying, and buttermilk dressing provides both richness and complementary tang.

**Yield: 6 to 8 servings**

4 medium green tomatoes, cut in ¼-inch slices

1 tablespoon kosher salt, plus more for sprinkling

1 teaspoon freshly ground black pepper

2 large eggs, beaten

¼ cup milk or cream

1 cup all-purpose flour

2 to 3 cups panko bread crumbs

¾ cup vegetable oil, plus more as needed

1. Lay the tomato slices on a platter and season both sides with the salt and pepper.

2. Beat the eggs and milk together in a small bowl and transfer to a shallow dish.

3. Place the flour and panko in their own separate, shallow dishes.

4. Arrange your three-stage breading assembly line (see note) in this order: sliced tomatoes, flour, egg wash, then panko. Have a dry tray or plate ready to hold the breaded tomatoes until you are ready to fry them.

5. Place the seasoned tomatoes in the flour a few pieces at a time and coat well. Dip the floured tomato slices into the egg wash and thoroughly coat on both sides, then transfer to the panko, pressing the slices into the breading to ensure a nice, even coating. Remove the slices from the panko and place on the dry tray. Bread all the tomatoes before you start frying. Covered loosely and refrigerated, breaded tomatoes will keep for a few hours before frying without negatively affecting the final product.

*(Continued)*

6. Heat the oil in a heavy, 10- to 12-inch sauté pan over medium-high heat. When the oil is shimmering, fry the tomatoes a few pieces at a time without crowding the pan. Fry for about 2 minutes on each side or until they are golden brown. Carefully remove the tomatoes from the pan with tongs and drain on paper towels. As you remove the hot tomatoes from the pan, season with a little sprinkle of salt. Add more oil to the pan and repeat the process until all the tomatoes have been fried.

7. Serve warm with the Buttermilk Dressing (recipe follows).

**NOTE:** Standard three-stage breading is a useful technique to bread almost anything. It consists of flour, an egg wash, and then the breading appropriate for your particular dish. The three steps combined give the end product a consistent breading that will stick to the product and not fall off during the cooking process. The flour makes the egg stick, the egg make the breading stick. Skip a step and the breading just won't adhere as well. Two things to remember when making and using a three-stage breading station: First, use a large, shallow dish for each of the three stages so you have room to coat multiple pieces of product at once without making a huge mess; and second, use one hand for the flour and final breading stage and the other for the egg stage. If you use the same hand going back and forth from the dry to the wet ingredients, within a few pieces you won't be able to recognize your own hand.

## Buttermilk Dressing

**Yield: about 1½ cups dressing**

¾ cup mayonnaise

½ cup buttermilk

¼ cup sour cream

2 teaspoons red wine vinegar

Juice and zest of 1 lemon

2 tablespoons chopped scallions

2 tablespoons chopped fresh parsley

1 teaspoon kosher salt

½ teaspoon Hattie's Hot Rub (page 141) or commercial Creole seasoning

Pinch of cayenne pepper

1. Combine all the ingredients in a medium bowl and blend with a whisk.

2. Buttermilk dressing will keep for 7 to 10 days, stored in an airtight container under refrigeration.

# Savory BBQ Shrimp

I have been making this dish in one form or another for virtually my entire career. One of my first jobs as a line cook was at Ponti Seafood Grill in Seattle, Washington. Ponti's longtime chef, Alvin Binuya, has helped define Pacific Northwest cuisine for the past 25 years. Alvin, who has been my boss, friend, and mentor, drew inspiration from many sources. In this particular instance, it was a trip to New Orleans. I have tweaked this recipe and its application over the years, but one constant is that, despite the name, it has nothing to do with BBQ in the traditional sense.

The shrimp marinade is quite potent on its own, but with the addition of cream and butter it mellows into a rich, earthy, and slightly sweet sauce with a pleasant spice kick. At Hattie's I've served it with crusty French bread, over creamy grits, or even over field greens as a warm salad. The sauce is rich, so whatever you serve it with becomes a vehicle for the sauce. You can make the finished dish right away, but the shrimp will be better if it's allowed to marinate for at least a few hours.

*(Continued)*

**Yield: serves 4 as an appetizer or 2 as an entrée**

2 tablespoons Seasoning Mix (recipe follows)

3 tablespoons chopped garlic

2 tablespoons soy sauce

2 tablespoons honey

2 tablespoons freshly squeezed lemon juice

¼ cup olive oil

1 pound wild gulf shrimp (21/25 or 16/20 count), shelled and deveined

3 tablespoons chopped fresh parsley

½ cup heavy cream

½ cup (1 stick) unsalted butter, at room temperature

1. Combine the Seasoning Mix, garlic, soy sauce, honey, and lemon juice in a blender or food processor.

2. Drizzle the olive oil into the processor or blender with the machine running. The goal is to emulsify the oil into the other ingredients, so go slowly and stop the machine when all the oil has been added.

3. Transfer the sauce to a medium bowl and add the shrimp and parsley. Stir until the shrimp are completely covered with the sauce. Marinate in the refrigerator for at least a few hours or overnight.

4. Pour the cream over the shrimp and mix evenly.

5. Transfer the shrimp mixture to a large, heavy sauté pan and bring to a simmer over medium-high heat, stirring occasionally.

6. When the cream is bubbling and the edges of the shrimp are turning pink, lower the heat to medium-low and begin adding the butter in 1- to 2-tablespoon increments while continuously shaking the pan. Allow each addition of butter to emulsify into the mixture before adding the next. This process should take 3 to 4 minutes.

7. Serve with crusty bread to mop up the sauce or over creamy grits.

## Seasoning Mix

**Yield: about 1 cup seasoning**

¼ cup freshly ground black pepper

2 tablespoons cayenne pepper

2 tablespoons Cajun seasoning

2 tablespoons salt

2 tablespoons dried whole thyme

2 tablespoons dried rosemary leaves

2 tablespoons crushed red pepper flakes

1 tablespoon onion powder

1 teaspoon dried oregano

Combine all the ingredients in a container with a tight-fitting lid and shake vigorously to blend. Will keep for months stored in an airtight container at room temperature.

## Crab Cakes with Sweet Corn Relish and Lime Mayo

The magic bullet of great cooking, as all the chefs I worked for pounded into my head, is to start with the best ingredients and then don't screw them up. In this case we start with high-quality lump or super lump crabmeat and add just enough of the right ingredients to enhance the natural flavor and texture of the crab. Too much binder and too much mixing will make a goopy crab-flavored bread ball, not a crab cake. Crab cakes are on the menu year-round at Hattie's, but we change the accompaniment to reflect the seasons. This is a popular summer variation with a simple but delicious sweet corn and bell pepper relish and a lime mayonnaise. The corn and peppers have only a 30-minute commute from Albert Sheldon's farm in Salem, New York, to our kitchen in Saratoga and usually we get them the day they are picked. You could serve this dish as a lunch or light dinner or as a first course for a more formal dinner party. The crab cakes are also great by themselves with just a squeeze of lemon.

*(Continued)*

**Yield: 6 to 8 crab cakes**

1 pound lump or super lump crabmeat

2 tablespoons olive oil

2 tablespoons finely chopped onion

2 tablespoons seeded and finely chopped red bell pepper

2 tablespoons seeded and finely chopped green bell pepper

2 tablespoons finely chopped celery

¼ cup mayonnaise

1 large egg, beaten

Juice and zest of 1 lemon

1 tablespoon chopped fresh parsley

1 tablespoon chopped scallions

1 teaspoon Old Bay Seasoning

2 teaspoons kosher salt

½ teaspoon freshly ground black pepper

2½ cups fresh or panko bread crumbs, divided

½ cup vegetable or olive oil, plus more if needed

1. Place the crabmeat in a small bowl and gently pull apart with a spoon.

2. Heat the olive oil in a small sauté pan over medium-high heat. When the oil is shimmering, add the onion, peppers, and celery and sauté for 1 minute. Remove from the heat and set aside to cool.

3. Add the mayonnaise, egg, lemon juice, and lemon zest to the crabmeat and gently fold the ingredients together with a rubber spatula. Add the parsley, scallions, Old Bay, salt, black pepper, and cooled vegetables and fold gently into the crab mixture. Keep as many lumps intact as possible, folding only enough to combine all the ingredients.

4. Sprinkle ½ cup of the bread crumbs over the crab mixture and fold a few more times so they are evenly dispersed. Then let the mixture sit for 5 minutes (see note).

5. Put the remaining 2 cups of bread crumbs in a shallow pan or bowl.

6. Scoop about ¼ to ⅓ cup of the crab mixture into the pan of bread crumbs. Press down lightly on the cake so the crumbs adhere to the bottom, then flip the cake over to coat the other side. Lift the crab cake from the bread crumbs and gently compress the cake between your hands to form a rough hockey-puck shape and set aside. Repeat the process until all the cakes are breaded.

7. Heat the oil in a large, heavy or nonstick sauté pan over medium heat. When the oil is shimmering, place the crab cakes in the pan, being careful not to crowd the pan (work in batches, if necessary). The oil should be gently bubbling up the sides of the crab cakes. The bread will soak up some of the oil, so you may need to add a little more oil while cooking. Cook for 2 to 3 minutes on each side, or until the crab cakes are golden brown, crispy, and hot in the middle.

8. Remove the crab cakes from the pan and place them on paper towels to drain. Repeat the process until all the crab cakes are cooked.

## Sweet Corn Relish

This recipe makes more than you will need for 6 to 8 crab cakes, but you will enjoy having it to accompany grilled meats. Stored in an airtight container under refrigeration, the relish will last for weeks.

1.  Combine the peppers, onion, celery, garlic, sugar, vinegar, water, and spices in a 4-quart stainless-steel saucepot.

2.  Bring the mixture to a boil over high heat. Lower the heat to maintain a simmer for 10 minutes. Add the corn kernels and continue to simmer for 5 minutes.

3.  Remove the pot from the heat and allow to cool completely before use. Serve chilled or at room temperature.

**Yield: about 6 cups relish**

½ cup seeded and finely chopped green bell pepper

½ cup seeded and finely chopped red bell pepper

½ cup finely chopped onion

½ cup finely chopped celery

5 garlic cloves, finely chopped

½ cup sugar

1 cup cider vinegar

1 cup water

1 teaspoon mustard seeds

½ teaspoon celery seeds

½ teaspoon red pepper flakes

¼ teaspoon ground turmeric

6 cups corn kernels (from 7 to 8 ears)

## Lime Mayonnaise

**Yield: about 1 cup mayonnaise**

1 cup mayonnaise

Juice and zest of 1 lime

Pinch of kosher salt

Pinch of freshly ground black pepper

Combine the lime juice and zest with the mayonnaise in a small bowl and season with salt and pepper to taste.

# Deviled Eggs

There are hundreds of deviled egg recipes, and many of them have some pretty wacky ingredients. I am of the mind that simple is best when it comes to deviled eggs. This recipe does just enough to push the egg up on the pedestal where it should be. If you're going to have problems with deviled eggs, it's usually because of how you boil them. Either the outer layer of the egg yolk turns gray, the shell sticks to the egg when you try to peel it, or both. This recipe will solve those problems. You can store the peeled eggs in the refrigerator in an airtight container or sealable bag for a couple of days before you devil them, if you wish.

**Yield: 24 deviled eggs; 6 to 8 servings**

12 large eggs

½ cup plus ½ teaspoon kosher salt, divided

¼ cup mayonnaise

1 tablespoon freshly squeezed lemon juice

½ teaspoon Worcestershire sauce

½ teaspoon Hattie's Hot Sauce or other Louisiana-style hot sauce

¼ teaspoon dry mustard

2 tablespoons chopped fresh chives

Pinch of paprika

1. Carefully place the eggs in the bottom of a 2-quart saucepot with a lid. Fill the pot with cold water, covering the eggs by at least an inch, and add ½ cup of the salt. This may seem like a lot of salt, but it will help prevent the inner membrane of the shell from sticking to the cooked egg white, making the eggs easier to peel. It will not make the eggs salty, I promise.

2. Cover the pot and bring the water to a boil over high heat. Once the water comes to a boil, remove the pot from the heat and allow the eggs to sit in the hot water for 12 minutes.

3. Carefully place the pot in the sink and run cold water in the pot until the eggs are cool enough to handle. The cold water will stop the cooking process, preventing the eggs from overcooking, which is what causes that gray layer on the yolks. As soon as the eggs are cool enough to handle, peel them under a slow stream of running water.

4. Cut the eggs in half lengthwise. Scoop the yolks out with a teaspoon into a small mixing bowl.

5. Add the mayonnaise, lemon juice, Worcestershire, hot sauce, dry mustard, and remaining ½ teaspoon of salt. Combine the ingredients with a fork, pushing the yolks against the sides and bottom of the bowl, breaking up any clumps of egg yolk. Scrape everything

*(Continued)*

back into the middle of the bowl and repeat until thoroughly combined and smooth.

6.  Scoop about 1 tablespoon of the yolk mixture into each egg white half and place on a platter (see note).

7.  Garnish with the chives and a little dusting of paprika.

**NOTE:** For a more refined look, you can load a pastry or cake-decorating bag fitted with a star tip and pipe the yolk mixture into the egg white halves.

## Andouille and Cheddar-Stuffed Mushrooms

As much as I hate to admit it, I suppose all the years spent in high-end kitchens has made me guilty, at times, of being a food snob. So, stuffed mushrooms are not something that I would typically order or even think about, for that matter. I'm quite sure that the last time I stuffed a mushroom was in culinary school for Chef Antoine Flurrie's skill class. So, when a former sous chef, Greg Hoffman, made some of these tasty little bites for a special one night, I was a bit skeptical. Now I'm a big boy, and despite what my friends, family, and co-workers might say, I can admit when I am wrong, and for the record I was wrong. These mushrooms were not the banquet tragedy I envisioned. They were tasty and sold out every time we ran them, so we put them on the menu. The fact that they are easy to make and can be made in advance

*(Continued)*

makes them a great party appetizer. Make sure you use fresh bread crumbs. Dried or store-bought will not give the same results.

**Yield: 20 to 30 mushrooms; serves 4 to 6**

1½ pounds large cremini or white button mushrooms

½ pound finely chopped andouille sausage

1 cup grated extra-sharp cheddar cheese

1 cup mayonnaise

½ cup chopped scallions

¼ cup chopped fresh parsley

½ teaspoon Old Bay Seasoning

½ teaspoon kosher salt

¼ teaspoon freshly ground black pepper

2 cups fresh bread crumbs (see note)

1. Preheat oven to 425°F.

2. Remove the stems from the mushrooms and cut a thin slice off the top of each mushroom so they will sit flat on a baking tray with the cavity facing up. You can discard the stems and trimmings or save them for chicken or vegetable stock.

3. Combine the sausage, cheese, mayonnaise, scallions, parsley, and seasonings in a medium bowl and blend together with a fork until well combined. Add the bread crumbs and blend in.

4. Stuff the cavity of the mushroom caps with a generous mound of stuffing and place them on a baking sheet, cut side down.

5. Bake for 10 to 15 minutes or until the mushrooms are cooked and the stuffing has browned.

**NOTE:** The easiest way to make fresh bread crumbs is to toss several slices of bread in a food processer or blender and pulse until finely chopped. Two slices makes about ½ cup of bread crumbs.

## Chicken Livers with Caramelized Onions and Bacon

I doubt there are many restaurants left that serve sautéed chicken livers. You might find them all gussied up, turned into pâté or formed into a terrine, but rarely are they out in the open, standing on their own. This recipe is straightforward and pairs chicken livers with their two best friends, bacon and onions.

*(Continued)*

**Yield: 4 servings**

## *Livers:*

12 ounces chicken livers, cleaned and trimmed (see note)

2 cups milk (optional)

½ cup all-purpose flour

2 teaspoons kosher salt

½ teaspoon freshly ground black pepper

½ cup olive oil, plus more as needed

## *Bacon and onions:*

1 tablespoon olive oil

4 slices smoked bacon, cut into ½-inch pieces

2 cups thinly sliced onion

½ teaspoon kosher salt

¼ teaspoon freshly ground black pepper

1 cup chicken stock, store-bought or homemade (page 253)

1 tablespoon chopped fresh rosemary

1 tablespoon chopped fresh thyme

1 tablespoon chopped fresh sage

2 tablespoons chopped fresh parsley

1. **Inspect and trim the livers:** Rinse under cold running water and drain in a colander. If you're going to soak the livers in milk, do this the night before or the morning of (see note).

2. **Prepare the bacon and onions:** Heat the olive oil in a 10-inch sauté pan over medium heat. Cook the bacon until the fat is rendered and the bacon is browned and just turning crisp, 15 to 20 minutes. Remove the bacon from the pan with a slotted spoon and drain on a paper towel.

3. Add the onion to the bacon drippings. Season with the salt and pepper and cook over medium heat for 20 to 25 minutes, stirring frequently until the onion turns a deep golden brown. Remove from the pan with a slotted spoon and set aside.

4. **Cook the livers:** Spread the flour in a pie dish or small baking pan. Season the livers with the salt and pepper and dredge them heavily, a few at a time, in the flour until they are completely covered with an even coat of flour. Coat all the livers before you begin to sauté them.

5. Heat the olive oil in a large, heavy, or nonstick sauté pan over medium-high heat.

6. When the oil is simmering, shake off any excess flour and carefully place the livers in the pan, making sure you do not crowd the pan (cook them in batches, if necessary). Sauté the livers for 3 to 4 minutes on each side, or until they are deep brown and fully cooked. You might need to change out the oil to keep the flour that falls off the livers from burning in the pan.

7. Remove the livers from the pan with a slotted spoon and keep warm. Discard the oil and any flour that is on the bottom, then wipe out the pan with a paper towel.

8. Return the pan to the heat and add the bacon and caramelized onion. Cook for 2 minutes over medium heat or until the bacon is crisp and the onion is hot. Add the chicken stock, rosemary, thyme, and sage. Increase the heat and bring the chicken stock to a simmer. Reduce by half.

9. Add the livers back to the pan. Cook the livers for 1 to 2 minutes, just to make sure they are hot.

10. Garnish with the parsley and serve plain or over some white or brown rice.

**NOTE:** Chicken livers are generally bound together with connective tissue and occasionally have a green sac hanging off the side. Separate the individual lobes if the livers are large and trim away any connective tissue. The green sac is the gall bladder and should be removed. Some people find that soaking the livers in milk for a few hours or overnight will tame their inherent liverocity. I find that, with most people, there is very little gray area when it comes to livers, and if you don't like the taste of liver, no amount of milk is going to change your mind.

# Pimento Cheese

Pimento cheese is the peanut butter of the South. This super easy cheese spread is a perennial favorite among Southerners and will be found at picnics and lunches across the region. It's incredibly versatile and can be spread on sandwiches, used as a dip for crudités, stuffed into celery ribs, scooped in a bowl and spread on crackers, or if you're like me, a spoon will do nicely as well.

My family, most of whom grew up around Winston-Salem, North Carolina, takes its pimento cheese very seriously. So much so, that a few years ago during a family reunion, we were debating the various ways to make pimento cheese and the discussion soon turned into an all-out, no-holds-barred pimento cheese battle. To keep the peace, we declared it a draw, all of us smart enough to realize that the real benefit of the contest was not declaring a winner, but ensuring that we had plenty of pimento cheese for the rest of the week.

Pimento cheese is one of those indigenous regional foods that, while enjoying widespread popularity in the South, is virtually unknown in other parts of the country. This has certainly been my experience at Hattie's over the years. I have tried to spread the gospel of its merits with only limited success.

When we opened Hattie's Chicken Shack a few years ago, I thought I finally had the right venue to bring pimento cheese to the masses. I put a toasted pimento cheese sandwich on the menu, thinking that kids would love it and that there might be just enough southbound snowbirds exposed to pimento cheese for it to get a foothold. Not the case. There were a few loyalists like me who loved it, but after many months of sluggish sales, it sadly had to go. I still have not given up the fight, and we now serve it in a crock with toast points at the original restaurant for brunch. I also slip it onto catering menus as often as I can.

**Yield: about 2 cups pimento cheese**

1 pound extra-sharp cheddar cheese, grated

½ cup mayonnaise

¼ cup sliced pimentos with their juice (about 1 [4-ounce] jar)

⅛ cup onion, grated with the juice

½ teaspoon kosher salt

¼ teaspoon freshly ground black pepper

1. Combine all the ingredients in a medium bowl and blend together with a spoon or rubber spatula.

2. Pimento cheese will keep for 7 to 10 days in an airtight container under refrigeration.

soups, stews, and
food served in a Bowl

# Brisket Chili

**Yield: 10 servings**

5 pounds beef brisket, cut into ½-inch pieces

¼ cup kosher salt

1 tablespoon freshly ground black pepper

½ cup vegetable oil, plus more as needed

6 cups diced onion (4 to 6 onions)

8 garlic cloves, finely chopped

1 jalapeño chili, chopped

1 serrano chili, chopped

1 habanero chili, chopped

2 tablespoons ground cumin

2 tablespoons chili powder

2 tablespoons smoked or sweet paprika

2 tablespoons dried oregano

2 tablespoons dried rosemary

2 (12-ounce) bottles beer (nothing fancy—a pilsner or lager)

2 cups chicken or veal stock, store-bought or homemade (page 253 and 254)

6 ancho chilies, soaked in warm water for 30 minutes

1 (28-ounce) can whole tomatoes

4 chipotle chilies in adobo

1 cup chopped fresh cilantro

3 to 4 cups cooked pinto or black beans (optional)

A lot of thought and a considerable amount of skill and patience goes into making good chili. Many people approach chili with the same passion and dedication that BBQ aficionados approach BBQ. When you make chili, there is a tangible and magical transformation of the simple raw ingredients into the complex finished product.

I tend to gravitate toward meat-based chilis due to their texture and richness. At its core, chili is a braised dish, so you want to choose a cut of meat that lends itself to long, moist cooking. For example, such cuts as beef brisket, chuck, or pork shoulder would be appropriate, whereas strip steak or pork tenderloin would taste like sawdust.

This chili recipe uses a variety of hot peppers. The number and variety give the finished chili a balanced spiciness and depth of flavor. Spicy heat tolerance is a very personal thing, and I don't believe in making something hot just for the sake of being hot. You can alter the number of chilies up or down to suit your tolerance, but I think the amounts in the recipe are a good place to start. Typically I don't put beans in this recipe, but it will certainly do no harm to add them, so I have listed them as an optional ingredient.

1. Season the brisket pieces with the salt and black pepper. Heat the oil in an 8-quart stockpot over medium-high heat until it begins to smoke. Make sure the stockpot is ovenproof if you wish to finish cooking the chili in the oven. I recommend searing the beef in 4 or 5 smaller batches. If you crowd the pan, you will end up steaming the beef. The color from the seared beef will give the finished chili a rich brown color and a more complex flavor. Transfer each batch of seared beef to a bowl with a slotted spoon and add more oil to the pot, if necessary.

2. When the last batch of beef has nice color, leave it in the pot and add the onion, garlic, jalapeño, serrano, habanero, cumin, chili powder, paprika, oregano, and rosemary. Stir the mixture a couple of times, add the reserved beef and any juices that have accumulated, and stir again to thoroughly combine the ingredients.

*(Continued)*

Continue to cook for 2 to 3 minutes, scraping the bottom of the pan to dislodge any crusty bits that might have developed while searing the beef.

3. Add the beer and stock to the pot and stir until all the ingredients are well combined. Bring the mixture to a gentle simmer.

4. While you're waiting for the mixture to come to a simmer, purée the soaked ancho chilies, tomatoes, chipotles, and cilantro until smooth and add to the pot. Add the cooked beans if desired.

5. At this point, you have a choice. The chili is going to need to cook for 3 to 4 hours, or until the brisket is very tender. You can do this on the stovetop, uncovered, over low heat, stirring frequently to make sure that the chili does not scorch on the bottom, or you can cook it in the oven at 275° to 300°F. If you choose the oven, you will not need to stir as frequently because the heat will be more evenly distributed, coming from all around the pot and not just the from the bottom. With either method, you will need to check and stir the chili occasionally as it cooks to make sure it is not getting too dry. Add more water or stock, if necessary.

6. This chili will be good if you eat it the day you make it, but if your schedule allows, it will be much better a day or two after you make it. The sharp, intense flavors will mellow and develop complexity. I like to serve chili with a variety of toppings—usually diced red onion, fresh cilantro, grated cheese, sour cream, and tortilla chips.

# Steamed Clams with Saffron, Tomato, and Thyme

Clams are incredibly versatile. Shucked and eaten raw—delicious. They can be fried, baked, and grilled with excellent results, but my favorite method is steaming. It's the easiest and most efficient way to cook a bunch of clams, and the by-product is a wonderfully rich broth that's just waiting for a loaf of crusty bread. The broth starts with onion, garlic, tomato, saffron, and white wine, which blend with the clam juice as the clams begin to open. Toss in a healthy chunk of butter and grab the bread and a glass of sauvignon blanc. Littlenecks, middlenecks, and topnecks are the best size clams for steaming. Plan for about two dozen clams per person for an entrée, or one dozen for a first course.

*(Continued)*

**Yield: 4 to 8 servings**

50 hard-shell clams (½ bushel)

¼ cup extra-virgin olive oil

2 cups chopped onion

1 cup chopped tomato

¼ cup finely chopped garlic

2 teaspoons saffron threads

1½ cups white wine

¼ cup (½ stick) unsalted butter

4 sprigs fresh thyme

Bread, for serving

1. Rinse the clams in a colander under cold running water to remove any sand. Set aside.

2. Choose an 8-quart stockpot with a lid. Heat the olive oil in the stockpot over medium heat.

3. When the oil begins to shimmer, add the onion and sauté for 5 minutes or until the onion begins to turn translucent. Add the tomato, garlic, and saffron and cook for an additional 2 to 3 minutes.

4. Add white wine and the clams to the onion mixture. Cover the pot and bring the mixture to a boil over high heat.

5. Steam for about 5 minutes. Remove the lid, add the butter and thyme sprigs, and continue to steam, covered, for an additional 5 minutes or until all the clams have opened, about 10 minutes total.

6. Transfer the opened clams into a large bowl with a slotted spoon. If there are any stubborn clams that won't open, give them another minute or two in the boiling broth. If they still don't open, they were probably dead and should discarded.

7. Pour the hot broth carefully back over the clams and grab the bread.

## Macaroni and Cheese

I put macaroni and cheese on the menu the first winter after taking ownership of Hattie's. As the weather started getting colder, it just seemed like a big bowl of cheesy, bubbling, hot mac and cheese would be a great addition. It was an instant hit and now has an almost cultlike following. In the spring, we post a daily countdown so that people have time to get their fill before it disappears for the summer, and by the middle of August they are calling the restaurant to see when it will be available again. There is nothing fancy about the recipe. The trick is using really good extra-sharp cheddar cheese and keeping the contrasting textures of a creamy interior and a crispy exterior.

The key to the creamy texture is to keep the sauce and the pasta separate until you're just ready to put the pasta in the oven. What

*(Continued)*

works even better is to chill both the pasta and the sauce in the refrigerator for a few hours or overnight. When they are both completely cool, you can mix them no problem. If you mix hot or even warm cheese sauce with the shocked pasta and don't bake it right away, the pasta will absorb the sauce and the finished dish will be more mushy than creamy. The crispiness requires freshly made bread crumbs. The pulverized commercial variety will not provide the desired texture. Use whatever bread you have on hand, even if it's a little stale, but make the bread crumbs yourself.

**Yield: 6 to 8 servings**

3 tablespoons kosher salt, divided

1 pound elbow macaroni

¼ cup (½ stick) unsalted butter

½ cup all-purpose flour

3 cups milk

1 cup heavy cream

2 bay leaves

½ teaspoon freshly ground black pepper

¾ pound premium extra-sharp cheddar cheese, grated, divided

2 cups coarsely chopped fresh bread crumbs (from about 4 slices of bread)

½ cup chopped scallions

1. In an 8-quart saucepot, bring 4 quarts of water and 2 tablespoons of the salt to a boil. Cook the elbow macaroni until al dente, 5 to 8 minutes. Drain through a colander and shock with cold water to stop the cooking. Set aside.

2. Melt the butter in a 2-quart saucepot over low heat. Add the flour and mix with a whisk until the two are thoroughly combined. Continue to cook for 3 to 5 minutes. You are going for a blond roux, so watch the heat and pull it off the stove if it starts to get brown.

3. While whisking with the heat on low, add the milk, cream, bay leaves, the remaining tablespoon of salt, and the black pepper. Increase the heat to medium and bring the sauce to a simmer, whisking frequently.

4. Lower the heat to maintain a gentle simmer for about 10 minutes, whisking every few minutes. Remove the sauce from the heat.

5. Add ½ pound of the cheese, adjusting the seasoning to taste.

6. If you're going to bake and serve the mac and cheese immediately, mix the cooled pasta with the cheese sauce, transfer the mixed pasta to a 13 x 9 x 2-inch baking dish, and proceed to step 8.

7. If you're going to serve the mac and cheese at a later time, don't mix the cheese sauce and the pasta together until they are both totally cool or you're ready to bake. Then, mix the cold pasta with the cold cheese sauce in a large bowl. Transfer the mixture to a large sauté pan or stockpot and warm over medium-high heat,

stirring frequently, until it's hot and bubbly. You can add a touch of cream or milk to help loosen things up, if necessary. Transfer to a 13 x 9 x 2-inch baking dish.

8.  Mix the fresh bread crumbs with the remaining ¼ pound of cheese and cover the macaroni completely.

9.  Bake in a preheated 425°F oven until the macaroni is hot and the topping is golden brown, about 20 minutes. Garnish with the scallions.

# Red Beans and Rice

**Yield: 6 to 8 cups; 6 servings**

1 pound dried small red beans or red kidney beans

¼ cup olive oil

1 pound andouille sausage, tasso, or other smoked pork product (optional)

1 cup chopped onion

½ cup chopped celery

½ cup seeded and chopped red bell pepper

½ cup seeded and chopped green bell pepper

¼ cup chopped garlic

2 tablespoons kosher salt

1 teaspoon freshly ground black pepper

2 teaspoons smoked paprika

1 teaspoon onion powder

1 teaspoon garlic powder

½ teaspoon cayenne pepper

8 cups vegetable or chicken stock, store-bought or homemade (pages 256 and 253)

1 tablespoon fresh chopped rosemary

1 tablespoon fresh chopped thyme

Steamed white or brown rice, for serving

¼ cup chopped scallions

¼ cup chopped fresh parsley

Red beans and rice is a dish synonymous with New Orleans and Creole cuisine. As the story goes, it was traditionally served on Mondays with the leftover bits and pieces from the also traditional Sunday pork roast. While I would definitely agree that beans love pork, and I often serve our red beans and rice with a piece of grilled andouille sausage, the red beans alone are vegetarian. Hattie's is unapologetically a chicken shack, which means that we are not going to have a multitude of options for our vegetarian and vegan friends. However, this does not absolve us of a responsibility to offer a few delicious options for those patrons who abstain.

We compensate for the lack of smoked porky goodness with the flavorful Cajun trinity of onions, celery, and bell peppers, plus lots of garlic and plenty of herbs and spices. I prefer using small red beans or small red chili beans as opposed to the larger kidney beans found in many recipes.

1. Soak the beans in water overnight, then drain when you are ready to cook.

2. Heat the olive oil in an 8-quart stockpot over medium-high heat. If you are going to add any pork, now is the time.

3. Sauté the onion and celery for 5 minutes or until they begin to soften. Add the bell peppers and the garlic, season with the salt and black pepper, and cook for an additional 10 minutes. Stir the spices into the vegetables and add the soaked and drained red beans.

4. Add the stock, increase the heat to high, and bring the mixture to a simmer, stirring occasionally. Once the beans come to a simmer, lower the heat to maintain a gentle simmer. Allow the red beans to cook for 60 to 90 minutes, stirring occasionally, until they are tender and creamy.

5. Add the fresh rosemary and thyme at the end of the cooking time. Serve over steamed white or brown rice and garnish with the scallions and parsley.

# Chicken and Dumplings

Chicken and dumplings, along with macaroni and cheese, was one of the first things I added to the menu after taking the reins at Hattie's. A staple in Southern cafés, it just seemed to fit the direction I was going with the menu. The comfort food classic has been on the menu ever since. This version is thickened slightly with pan roux and is similar to a chicken potpie filling with boiled Baking Powder Dumplings rather than piecrust. It's a great option on a cold fall or winter day. You can make the dumplings while the chicken is cooking or while you're waiting for it to cool enough to bone. Just leave the dough covered so it doesn't dry out.

**Yield: about 1½ gallons; 10 to 12 servings**

1 (3- to 4-pound) pound chicken

12 cups chicken stock, store-bought or homemade (page 253)

2 bay leaves

1 teaspoon dried thyme

1 teaspoon dried rosemary

½ teaspoon dried tarragon

½ cup (1 stick) unsalted butter

2 cups chopped onions

1 cup chopped celery

1 cup chopped carrot

1 cup chopped fennel (about 1 bulb)

2 tablespoons finely chopped garlic

1 tablespoon kosher salt

1 teaspoon freshly ground black pepper

1 cup all-purpose flour

1 batch Baking Powder Dumplings (recipe follows)

1 tablespoon chopped fresh rosemary

1 tablespoon chopped fresh thyme

1 tablespoon chopped fresh parsley

1. Place the chicken, chicken stock, and dried herbs in an 8-quart stockpot and bring to a boil. Lower the heat to a low simmer and cook for 45 minutes or until the chicken is tender and beginning to fall apart.

2. Carefully remove the chicken from the pot and set aside. When the chicken is cool enough to handle, remove the skin and bones and set the meat aside.

3. Strain the fortified chicken stock into another container and set aside. Rinse and dry the 8-quart pot and return it to the burner.

4. Melt the butter in the stockpot over medium heat and sauté the onions, celery, carrots, fennel, garlic, salt, and pepper for 5 minutes. Sprinkle the flour over the vegetables, lower the heat to low, and continue to cook for an additional 3 minutes, stirring frequently.

5. Pour 4 cups of the reserved chicken stock over the vegetables and bring to a simmer, stirring constantly. Add the remaining chicken stock and cooked chicken and bring the mixture to a gentle boil, then lower the heat to low.

6. Simmer on low heat for at least 10 minutes to be sure you have cooked away any floury taste.

7. Add the dumplings and cook for an additional 10 minutes or until the dumplings are fully cooked. Stir in the fresh herbs and serve.

# Baking Powder Dumplings

1½ cups plus 2 tablespoons
all-purpose flour, divided

2 teaspoons baking powder

1 teaspoon sugar

1 teaspoon salt

1 cup milk

1. In a small bowl, combine 1½ cups of the flour and the baking powder, sugar, and salt.

2. Add the milk and blend with a large spoon until it is fully incorporated. The dough will be wet and sticky.

3. Sprinkle the remaining 2 tablespoons of flour on your work surface and turn the dough onto the flour. Flip the dough over a couple of times so it has a light coating of flour to help prevent it from sticking to your hands.

4. With your fingertips, pull and fold the dough over from the twelve o'clock to the six o'clock position and then push down with the heel of your hand.

5. Turn the dough a quarter turn and repeat the previous step. Continue this pattern 5 or 6 times, until the dough is smooth, soft, and no longer sticks to your hands. You do not want to overwork the dough as it will overdevelop the gluten and result in tough dumplings. Let the dough rest for 5 to 10 minutes before cutting and cooking.

6. To form the individual dumplings, cut off a chunk of the dough and roll it out with your hands on your work surface so that you have a rope about the diameter of a quarter, then cut it into ½-inch pieces. To cook, drop into the Chicken and Dumplings broth on page 76 and follow the instructions for step 7.

# Crawfish Étouffée

In this dish I diverge from what is considered classical or even proper. Étouffée, which literally means "to smother," is a stewlike dish served over rice. Étouffée is generally made with a blond roux that provides thickening power but little flavor. I really like the nutty undertones that a darker roux provides. In this recipe, we use a light brown roux that both thickens and provides depth to the flavor of the finished dish. Crawfish is certainly the most popular protein for étouffée, but an equal amount of crab or shrimp would also be delicious. Unless you live along the Gulf, you are not likely to find crawfish tails in the grocery store, but your fishmonger should be able to order them or they can be ordered online. Generally they are shipped frozen, cooked and packed in their own fat, called "butter."

*(Continued)*

**Yield: about 12 cups;**
**6 servings**

¾ cup vegetable oil

½ cup all-purpose flour

2 cups chopped onion

1 cup chopped celery

1 cup seeded and chopped red bell pepper

1 cup seeded and chopped green bell pepper

2 tablespoons chopped garlic

2 teaspoons kosher salt

1 teaspoon freshly ground black pepper

8 cups shellfish or fish stock, store-bought or homemade (pages 258 and 257)

2 teaspoons dried thyme

2 teaspoons paprika

¼ teaspoon cayenne pepper

2 bay leaves

2 pounds crawfish tails in their "butter" (see headnote)

Steamed rice, for serving

¼ cup chopped fresh parsley

¼ cup chopped scallions

1. Heat the oil in an 8-quart stockpot over medium heat. Whisk in the flour and cook over medium-low heat, stirring frequently, for 10 minutes or until the roux is the color of peanut butter.

2. Add the onion, celery, bell peppers, and garlic to the roux and season with the salt and black pepper. Cook for 10 minutes or until the vegetables are beginning to get soft.

3. Add the stock, thyme, paprika, cayenne, and bay leaves and bring to a simmer, stirring frequently. Once the étouffée has thickened, lower the heat to maintain a gentle simmer and cook for 15 minutes, stirring occasionally, to let all the flavors blend.

4. Add the crawfish tails and cook for about 3 minutes or until the crawfish is hot.

5. Serve over steamed rice and garnish with the parsley and scallions.

# Jambalaya

Jambalaya, along with gumbo and red beans and rice, make up the triple crown of classic New Orleans/Louisiana dishes. It's a dish of humble origins made with varying combinations of rice, meat, seafood, vegetables, and aromatics all cooked together to form a delicious and festive one-pot meal. It is generally accepted that jambalaya most closely resembles the Spanish dish paella; however, every culture in the melting pot of New Orleans has a similar dish, from West Africa's jolluf, to the French pilau, to the arroz con (anything) of Latin America and the Caribbean.

Like gumbo, there are Cajun versions sometimes called "brown" jambalayas, which are typically spicier, stock-based, and made without tomatoes. Creole jambalayas are tomato-based and commonly referred to as "red" jambalaya. At Hattie's we make a Creole jambalaya with chicken, shrimp, and andouille sausage. Like gumbo, it's ripe for

*(Continued)*

**Yield: 10 servings**

½ cup olive oil (or that bacon or duck fat you have been saving in the back of the fridge)

½ pound boneless, skinless chicken thighs or breasts, cut into 1-inch pieces

1 pound andouille sausage, cut lengthwise, then crosswise into ½-inch slices

½ pound smoked ham, cut into ½-inch cubes

3 cups chopped onions

1 cup chopped celery

1 cup seeded and chopped red bell pepper

1 cup seeded and chopped green bell pepper

1 cup chopped fresh tomato

¼ cup chopped garlic

½ cup chopped scallions, divided

1 teaspoon kosher salt

½ teaspoon freshly ground black pepper

1 tablespoon paprika

2 teaspoons dark chili powder

½ teaspoon cayenne pepper

1 teaspoon dried thyme

1 teaspoon dried oregano

1 teaspoon dried rosemary

2 bay leaves

1 (28-ounce) can diced or crushed tomatoes

3 cups chicken or shellfish stock, store-bought or homemade (pages 253 and 258)

2½ cups uncooked long-grain white rice, rinsed

½ pound large shrimp (16/20 count), peeled and cut in half lengthwise

¼ cup chopped fresh parsley

experimentation, so once you get the basic process down, play around and see what you can come up with.

This recipe is a variation of the jambalaya we serve at the restaurant, but tailored for the home cook. While not a dish for one, you can easily cut this recipe in half if you're not cooking for a crowd. A lot of flavor building goes on here, so keep that in mind as you read the recipe and prepare your jambalaya.

1. Choose an ovenproof 8-quart Dutch oven or heavy stockpot with a lid and position a rack in the lower portion of your oven so that the pot will fit comfortably in the oven with the lid on. Preheat oven to 350°F.

2. Heat the oil or fat of choice over medium-high heat. When the oil is beginning to smoke, add the chicken pieces and sauté for 3 minutes.

3. Add the andouille sausage and ham and sauté for 5 minutes or until the sausage begins to brown.

4. Add the onions, celery, bell peppers, fresh tomato, garlic, and ¼ cup of the scallions and sauté for about 10 minutes or until the vegetables start to soften. Stir in the salt, spices, and dried herbs.

5. Add the canned tomatoes and stock and bring the mixture to a boil. Add the rice and, as soon as the mixture returns to a boil, put the lid on the pot and place it in the oven. Cook for 30 minutes (set a timer and no peeking).

6. After 30 minutes, remove the pot from the oven and spread the shrimp over the top of the jambalaya. Cover the pot and return it to the oven for an additional 10 minutes.

7. After your jambalaya has cooked for a total of 40 minutes, remove the pot from the oven and allow it to rest for an additional 10 minutes. Fluff the jambalaya, mix in the shrimp, and garnish with the remaining ¼ cup of scallions and the parsley.

# Gazpacho

When the weather gets hot and sticky, it's perfect weather for gazpacho. Gazpacho is a simple cold vegetable soup of Spanish origin. It's generally tomato based, with much variation and debate on the exact ingredients and the proper finished texture. For the past couple of decades, people have been taking wide latitude with the term *gazpacho*, using it to refer to any vegetable- or fruit-based soup that's at least partially pureed and served cold. This recipe is pretty standard and straightforward. The blend of tomatoes, cucumbers, peppers, and garlic is enriched with a little olive oil, thickened by a bit of bread, and balanced with a splash of sherry vinegar. Because this recipe is so simple, the quality of the finished soup is entirely dependent on the quality of the vegetables you choose. The tomatoes are especially important, so pick sweet, ripe heirloom tomatoes from your local farmers' market for best results.

**Yield: about 4 to 6 cups; 4 servings**

2 (½-inch-thick) slices French or Italian bread

1 cup water

2 pounds tomatoes, coarsely chopped

1 medium cucumber, peeled and coarsely chopped

½ green bell pepper, seeded and coarsely chopped

½ red bell pepper, seeded and coarsely chopped

2 garlic cloves

½ cup extra-virgin olive oil

1 to 2 tablespoons sherry vinegar

2 teaspoons kosher salt

½ teaspoon freshly ground black pepper

1. Soak the bread with the water in a small bowl and set aside.

2. Combine the chopped tomatoes, cucumbers, bell peppers, and garlic in a blender. Pulse the ingredients a couple of times, then add the bread and water. With the blender running, slowly drizzle the olive oil and vinegar into the vegetable mixture. Season with the salt and black pepper and continue to blend until you have the texture you desire.

3. Pour the soup into an airtight container and chill for at least 1 to 2 hours or until it's nice and cold.

4. Serve in bowls or cups. The garnish can be as simple as another drizzle of extra-virgin olive oil or some sliced radish, diced cucumber, or peppers.

# Stone Soup

There are as many variations of this soup as there are variations of the folktale it stems from. The exact story or even the exact recipe is not as important as the meaning behind it. The message in the story centers on the spirit of sharing, breaking bread with the people around you, making do, and being content with what you have.

A cook named Joe who worked for us for a brief time introduced me to this simple but deceptively complex-tasting soup. To take a barometer reading of Joe's skills, I asked him to make me a soup using some leftover mashed potatoes and whatever extra stuff we had lying around. Joe, who was Portuguese, said he had just the soup and launched into the story of the wandering friar and his stone, as he proceeded to make this delicious saffron-kissed soup with potatoes, sausage, and kale. This is a great way to use leftover mashed potatoes, but the soup is just as easily made with raw potatoes.

**Yield: 8 cups; 4 to 6 servings**

¼ cup olive oil

12 ounces chorizo sausage, cut in half lengthwise, then crosswise into ½-inch slices

2 cups chopped onions

2 garlic cloves, finely chopped

½ teaspoon saffron threads

2 bay leaves

2 teaspoons kosher salt

2½ cups mashed potatoes, or 2 to 3 large potatoes, peeled or scrubbed and cut into ½-inch cubes

2 cups chopped kale

4 cups chicken or vegetable stock, store-bought or homemade (pages 253 and 256)

1. Heat the oil in a heavy 4-quart saucepot over medium-high heat.

2. When the oil is shimmering, add the chorizo and cook for 5 minutes, or until the sausage begins to brown.

3. Add the onions, garlic, saffron, bay leaves, and salt. Lower the heat to medium and sauté for 10 minutes or until the onion is soft.

4. Add the potatoes, kale, and stock.

5. If you're using leftover mashed potatoes, break up the mass of potato with a spoon or whisk to help the stock absorb the potato. The finished soup will be a little thicker and have a uniform texture, as the potato will absorb all the stock. If you use raw potatoes, cook until the potatoes are falling apart and thickening the broth slightly. The overall appearance will be more brothlike. Either way, you may need to add a little more stock to adjust the consistency and check the seasoning.

## Shrimp, Andouille, and Corn Gumbo

First, you make a little roux. There are a slew of Southern, Cajun, and Creole recipes that start with this phrase, and the Cajun-style gumbo we make at Hattie's is no exception. For my money, the depth of flavor and chocolaty color that dark roux provides is even more important than its thickening quality. Your reward for a carefully crafted dark roux is a rich and deeply flavorful gumbo.

Generally speaking, gumbos are most often made with seafood or various types of fowl and game ranging from chicken to venison. Most have andouille sausage or some other type of smoked pork product and fall into two categories: Cajun gumbos, which are spicier, stock-based, and thickened with dark roux and sometimes filé powder (ground sassafras leaves); and Creole gumbos, which are more delicately spiced, lighter in texture and flavor, generally seafood based, occasionally contain tomatoes, and are typically thickened with okra.

*(Continued)*

This gumbo contains shrimp and andouille and the seasonal addition of fresh sweet corn. It is more Cajun than Creole, but definitive lines between these two cuisines are hard to come by.

**Yield: 4 quarts; serves 8 to 10**

1 cup vegetable oil

1½ cups all-purpose flour

2 pounds andouille sausage, cut lengthwise, then crosswise into ½-inch slices

2 cups chopped onions

1 cup chopped celery

1 cup seeded and diced chopped red bell pepper

1 cup seeded and diced chopped green bell pepper

¼ cup finely chopped garlic

1 tablespoon chili powder

1 tablespoon paprika

1 teaspoon cayenne pepper

1 tablespoon dried rosemary

2 tablespoons dried thyme

2 tablespoons dried oregano

4 cups tomato juice

8 cups chicken stock, canned or homemade (page 253)

1 pound large shrimp (16/20 count), shelled and cut in half lengthwise

3 cups corn kernels, fresh or frozen

Steamed rice, for serving

¼ cup chopped scallions

¼ cup chopped fresh parsley

1. Heat the oil in a heavy 8-quart stockpot over medium heat. Whisk in the flour. Once combined, the mixture should look like wet sand. Continue to cook over medium-low heat, whisking frequently, for 30 to 45 minutes or until the roux is the color of dark chocolate. The darker the roux gets, the faster it may burn, so stay vigilant as the roux starts to darken. As soon as its color changes from milk chocolate to dark chocolate, pull it off the heat. If the roux burns, the game is over, you lost, and you have to start again. Now that you're staring at a perfect dark roux, return the pot to the burner over medium-low heat.

2. Add the andouille sausage and sauté for 2 to 3 minutes. Add the onion, celery, bell peppers, and garlic (see note) and cook for about 15 minutes. Add the spices and dried herbs and cook for 2 to 3 additional minutes.

3. Add the tomato juice and chicken stock and increase the heat to medium-high, bringing the gumbo to a vigorous simmer while stirring frequently.

4. Once the gumbo has come close to a boil, lower the heat to maintain a gentle simmer and cook for 20 to 30 minutes. This will ensure that the complex flavors of the gumbo have a chance to get friendly and any floury taste from the roux will have cooked out.

5. Add the shrimp and corn about 5 minutes before you are ready to serve the gumbo.

6. Serve over steamed rice and garnish with the chopped scallions and parsley.

**NOTE:** Because roux is a thickener and vegetables are mostly water, it stands to reason that at the point when you add the vegetables to the hot roux, the whole mixture may start to seize up. Don't panic. Reduce the heat to low and add some extra oil a little bit at a time until the mixture loosens up.

# Oceans, Rivers, and Ponds

# Fried Catfish with Tartar Sauce Two Ways

Catfish are found on every continent on earth except Antarctica and can survive where other less adaptable fish would perish. As a result, they are a popular food source around the world. In America, catfish can be caught in almost any lake, stream, or river, but the quality of wild catfish depends on the source. The flavor can vary from mildly sweet and pleasant to muddy and chemically. If the catfish you catch are from a clean lake or river, they're likely to taste great. Conversely, if you catch them in the bog next to the oil refinery, catch and release might be a better option. Although wild-caught fish from pristine waters is always going to be superior to the farm-raised version, the quality of farm-raised catfish is excellent and sustainable. Fried catfish is always on the menu at Hattie's, served simply with a couple kinds of tartar sauce and lemon wedges.

**Yield: 4 to 6 servings**

2 cups buttermilk

1 tablespoon hot sauce

4 (6- to 7-ounce) catfish fillets

½ cup all-purpose flour

1 cup cornmeal

2 tablespoons Hattie's Hot Rub (page 141) or commercial blackening spice

1 teaspoon kosher salt

1 cup vegetable oil, plus more if necessary

1 cup Tartar Sauce (recipes follow)

Lemon wedges, for serving

1. Combine the buttermilk and hot sauce in a medium bowl.

2. Add the catfish to the buttermilk and allow it to soak while you assemble the remaining ingredients.

3. In a shallow baking dish, combine the flour, cornmeal, hot rub, and salt.

4. Remove the catfish from the buttermilk, one fillet at time, and hold it over the bowl for a few seconds to allow the excess buttermilk to run back into the bowl. You want only a thin coating of buttermilk to help the breading stick to the fish.

5. Dredge the catfish fillet in the cornmeal mixture, covering completely and pressing lightly to ensure an even coating. Coat all the catfish before you start frying.

6. Heat the oil in a large, heavy sauté pan over medium heat. You want to have enough oil in the pan for it to come about halfway up the fillets. So, depending on the size of your pan, you may need a little more or less oil than the recipe calls for.

*(Continued)*

7. Without crowding, panfry a few of the catfish fillets for 3 to 4 minutes on each side or until golden brown. Carefully lift the catfish from the pan and drain on a paper towel. Add more oil to the pan, if necessary, and cook the remaining pieces of fish.

8. Serve with Tartar Sauce (reciepes below), whichever one you prefer, or maybe both, and the lemon wedges.

# Tartar Sauce Two Ways

This tartar sauce is great for any fried fish or really any fish dish you'd like to enhance with a creamy, lemony sauce. It's super easy to make and infinitely better than any store-bought variety. Refrigerated, it will last for about a week.

## Lemony Dill Tartar Sauce

Combine all the ingredients in a medium bowl and blend thoroughly.

## Creole Tartar Sauce

Use the recipe for Lemony Dill Tartar Sauce, omitting the dill and adding 1 teaspoon Hattie's Hot Rub or other Cajun seasoning and ½ teaspoon cayenne pepper.

**Yield: 1½ cups sauce**

1 cup mayonnaise

¼ cup chopped dill pickle

2 tablespoons capers

3 tablespoons freshly squeezed lemon juice

½ teaspoon Worcestershire sauce

½ teaspoon Hattie's Hot Sauce or other Louisiana-style hot sauce

¼ cup chopped scallions

2 tablespoons chopped fresh parsley

½ teaspoon fresh dill

¼ teaspoon kosher salt

¼ teaspoon freshly ground black pepper

## Pecan-Crusted Trout with Tomato Bacon Jam

I have a soft spot in my heart for trout. I started fly-fishing in my late teens, and over the years I have come to respect the trout and its ability to spit out my fly and swim away laughing. Ketchum and Sun Valley are trout-fishing meccas with multiple world-class trout streams surrounding the area. The Big Wood River, which runs straight through town, was so close to my condominium I could hear it from my bedroom. Wild trout is splendid to catch and eat, but farmed trout is fine. It's widely available, affordable, versatile, and sustainable. I serve it in a variety of styles, depending on the season, but the combination of pecan-crusted trout and tomato bacon jam is one of my favorites. The jam is also great on sandwiches, with cheese and crackers, or with eggs.

*(Continued)*

**Yield: 4 servings**

4 (8-ounce) whole trout fillets

2 teaspoons kosher salt

½ teaspoon freshly ground black pepper

4 cups finely crushed pecans (about 1 pound; see note)

¼ cup olive oil, plus more as needed

¼ cup Tomato Bacon Jam (recipe follows) per fillet

Lemon wedges, for serving

1. Preheat oven to 400°F.

2. Remove any fine bones from the trout that may have been missed during filleting. Place the fillets, skin side down, on a baking sheet and season with the salt and pepper. Sprinkle with enough of the crushed pecans to generously cover the flesh side of each trout fillet. Press down firmly on the pecans to help set them into the trout. Pick up the trout by the tail and let the loose pecans fall onto the pan. Lay the trout back on the pan and sprinkle more pecans over the trout, pressing them down as before. Repeat this process until the trout fillets are completely covered with pecans.

3. Heat the olive oil in a large, heavy sauté pan over medium-high heat.

4. When the oil is shimmering and just beginning to smoke, carefully lay the trout into oil 1 or 2 at a time, depending on the size of your pan. Cook for 3 to 4 minutes or until the pecan crust is golden brown.

5. Carefully remove the trout from the pan with a spatula and place on a baking sheet, pecan side up.

6. When all the trout has been seared, finish it in the oven for an additional 5 minutes. Top the trout with ¼ cup of Tomato Bacon Jam and a wedge of lemon.

**NOTE:** Finely chop the pecans in a food processor or crush them in a sealable bag with a mallet or the back of a pan. You want the pecans crushed to the point of looking like chunky pecan flour rather than small pecan pieces.

# Tomato Bacon Jam

**Yield: 3 cups jam**

½ pound bacon, cut into ½-inch pieces

1 cup washed and chopped leeks, white and light green portion only

1 pound fresh chopped tomatoes and their juice, or 2 (28-ounce) cans diced canned tomatoes, drained and rinsed

½ cup light brown sugar

2 tablespoons cider vinegar

½ teaspoon soy sauce

⅛ teaspoon red chili flakes

¼ teaspoon dry mustard

½ teaspoon salt

¼ teaspoon freshly ground black pepper

1. Render and brown the bacon in a large sauté pan over medium heat. When the bacon is browned, remove it from pan with a slotted spoon and drain on a paper towel.

2. Drain the bacon fat from of the pan, reserving ¼ cup.

3. Return the pan to the heat and sauté the leeks in the ¼ cup of reserved bacon fat over medium heat for 5 to 6 minutes or until they are starting to get soft.

4. Add the tomatoes, sugar, cider vinegar, soy sauce and spices to the leeks. Increase the heat to medium-high and bring the mixture to a boil, stirring frequently. Lower the heat to maintain a low simmer and cook slowly for 20 to 25 minutes, stirring occasionally.

5. Add the bacon back to the tomato mixture and continue to cook on low heat for another 20 to 30 minutes or until most of the liquid has evaporated and the mixture is thick and glossy.

6. The jam will last for about a week, stored in an airtight container under refrigeration.

# Crawfish Boil

There is no way I would have guessed that catching crawfish in the creek behind our house in San Diego—with hot dogs, paper clips, and string—would lead to hosting an annual Memorial Day crawfish festival on the other side of the country 30 years later. But life is strange, and sometimes that's just how things work out. Crawfish are little freshwater crustaceans that look a lot like mini lobsters and can be found in creeks and ponds almost anywhere in the country. Most commercial crawfish comes from Louisiana, and the season generally lasts from December through June, with the peak season running from March to May. They are typically sold live, graded by size, or cooked as shucked tails. I get all my crawfish from the Louisiana Crawfish Company. It is knowledgeable, easy to deal with, and grows an excellent product. Get the biggest size you can and plan on 2 pounds per person with all the fixings, or 3 to 4 pounds per person if you're just cooking crawfish. I know that might sound like a lot, but there's not much meat in a crawfish. What there is, however, packs a lot of flavor and a lot of fun. The wow factor of pouring a big pile of crawfish, corn, potatoes, and sausage onto a table covered with newspapers is huge. Watching everyone get down and dirty, cracking tails and sucking on crawfish heads, is priceless. Keep the crawfish spicy and the beer cold. *C'est bon! Laissez les bon temps rouler!*

*(Continued)*

**Yield: 10 servings**

About 5 gallons water

1 batch Hattie's Crawfish/
Shrimp Boil (recipe follows), or
commercial alternative

20 garlic cloves, peeled

20 pounds live crawfish

5 pounds small new potatoes,
washed but not peeled

12 ears corn, shucked and
halved

2 pounds andouille sausage or
kielbasa, cut into 2- to 3-inch
pieces

1. Fill an 8- to 10-gallon pot (see note) with the water. Add the crawfish/shrimp boil and the garlic. Cover the pot and bring to a boil over high heat. Lower the heat to maintain a gentle simmer for 30 to 40 minutes.

2. While the boil is simmering, prepare to clean the crawfish. You're going to need tongs or a pair of gloves, a colander, and two 4- to 5-gallon buckets.

3. The crawfish are going to come in plastic mesh bags. Leave them in the bags for now and give them a thorough rinse under cold running water. Fill one of your buckets with cold water and plunge the bag of crawfish a few times into the cold water. Repeat this process until the water is mostly clear. Place your colander in the sink and pour a manageable amount of crawfish from the bag into the colander. Live crawfish are very perishable, so expect to find a few that have died in transport. With tongs or gloved hands, discard any dead crawfish as well as any debris you may find and give them another rinse. Place the clean, live crawfish into the other bucket so they don't go running all over your kitchen while you sort and rinse the rest. All this may sound like a lot of work, but it's really half the fun. Wait for some of your guests to show up and make them join in. Tell them it's a rite of passage.

4. Bring your pot of water back to a boil, add the potatoes, and cook for 10 minutes. Add the corn and sausage and cook for another 5 minutes. Add your crawfish, cook for 5 minutes, then turn off the heat and allow the whole mixture to sit and soak for 10 minutes.

5. Drain and strain all the liquid out of the pot, then pour the contents of your pot onto a table covered with newspapers.

**NOTE:** The pots that are designed for frying turkeys generally come with a handled colander that is almost the same size as the pot, making straining the finished crawfish boil a snap. It's worth the small investment if you're cooking for a crowd. If you have scaled down the recipe for just a few people, you can also scale down the pot size and use a strainer to scoop out the crawfish and the vegetables.

**Yield: About 1 pound boil spices**

1 pound kosher salt

10 bay leaves, crushed

½ cup Old Bay Seasoning

¼ cup cayenne pepper

3 tablespoons paprika

2 tablespoons garlic powder

2 tablespoons onion powder

2 tablespoons freshly ground black pepper

1 tablespoon ground coriander

1 tablespoon ground allspice

1 tablespoon dried oregano

1 tablespoon dried thyme

1 tablespoon dry mustard

# Hattie's Crawfish/Shrimp Boil

Combine all the ingredients in a medium-size bowl and mix thoroughly. The boil spices will last for months, stored in an airtight container.

## How to Eat a Crawfish

1. Take a sip of beer and grab a crawfish.

2. Twist and pull the tail from the head and suck the juice out of the head.

3. Peel the first ring or two off the tail.

4. Grab the exposed tail meat with your teeth and pinch at the back of the tail; the meat should come right out.

5. Take sip of beer and repeat.

# Seared Sea Scallops with Grits, Watercress, and Brown Butter Balsamic Vinaigrette

While the Northwest has salmon on lockdown, the Northeast gets bragging rights in the scallop department. A good Northeast dry-pack scallop is amazingly sweet and tastes like the ocean. "What's a dry-pack scallop and how can I tell?" The term *dry-pack* refers to how the scallops are handled once they are brought onboard the boat. The better-quality "dry" scallop is harvested, shucked, and put in a can; that's it. Wet scallops are shucked and held in a solution of water and sodium tripolyphosphate to make them last longer. Sounds yummy, right? Let's be very clear: You do not want to eat wet scallops—they are difficult to sear and horribly inferior in every way. It's easy to tell the difference. Dry scallops are dry, while a strange, iridescent, milky liquid surrounds wet scallops. The other consideration is size. Typically, the bigger the scallop, the bigger the price. For this recipe, I would suggest 10/20s, but if your fishmonger has some big fatties and you want to spend the money, go for it. Scallops are rich, so figure on about 5 ounces per person.

Scallops cook quickly and should be eaten right away, so prepare the grits, vinaigrette, and vegetable components before cooking the scallops. Plan on about ¾ cup of cooked grits per person.

*(Continued)*

**Yield: 4 servings**

1 batch Basic Grits (page 173)

2 cups watercress leaves (about 2 bunches), plus more for serving

¼ cup olive oil

20 dry sea scallops (about 1¼ pounds)

1 teaspoon kosher salt

¼ teaspoon freshly ground white pepper

¼ cup Brown Butter Balsamic Vinaigrette (recipe follows)

2 cups grape or cherry tomatoes, halved

½ cup chopped scallions (about 1 bunch)

1. Prepare the grits according to their recipe and keep warm.

2. Pick the leaves from the watercress, discarding the bigger stems, and arrange a small circle of watercress in the middle of each plate.

3. Heat the olive oil in a large, heavy sauté pan over medium-high heat. Pat your scallops dry with a paper towel and season with the salt and pepper.

4. When the oil is shimmering and just about to smoke, carefully place the scallops in the pan, one at a time, being careful not to crowd the pan. If you don't have a pan big enough to cook all the scallops at once, cook them in batches.

5. Cook the scallops on one side, without moving them around, until they are turning golden brown on the bottom and sides, about 3 minutes. Carefully flip the scallops over and pull your pan off the heat. Leave the scallops in the pan for 1 to 2 minutes for medium rare, or a little longer for medium. I would not suggest cooking any scallop past medium. They can get tough and rubbery.

6. To serve, scoop a portion of the grits on top of the watercress. Arrange the scallops on top of the grits, pushing them down slightly so they stay put, and drizzle the vinaigrette over and around the plate. Garnish with the tomatoes, scallions, and a few more watercress leaves.

# Brown Butter Balsamic Vinaigrette

This is a great variation on the Brown Butter Lemon Vinaigrette (page 113). I first saw it used while working with Scott Staples in Seattle, just before moving to Saratoga. The reduced balsamic provides a nice counterpoint to the nutty butter but retains enough of the acidity to round out the flavors.

**Yield: about 1½ cups vinaigrette**

2 cups (4 sticks) unsalted butter

½ cup finely chopped shallot (3 to 4 shallots)

¾ cup balsamic vinegar

1 teaspoon kosher salt

½ teaspoon freshly ground black pepper

1. Heat the butter in a small saucepot over medium heat until the milk solids separate and fall to the bottom of the pot. Reduce the heat to low and continue to cook until the milk solids turn dark brown and give the butter a nutty aroma. The butter should be as dark as it can be without burning. This will take 20 to 30 minutes. When the butter is dark and nutty, remove from the heat and allow to cool.

2. Place the shallots and vinegar in a separate saucepot and reduce by half—to about ⅓ cup—over medium heat.

3. Once the butter has cooled (see note), combine with the shallots and reduced vinegar and season with the salt and pepper.

NOTE: If you add the vinegar to the hot butter, it will boil over and cause a big mess. If you make that mistake with the pot still on the burner and it foams over onto an open flame or electric burner, you could have a small grease fire, so be careful. Once the two parts are blended, you can reheat the sauce over low heat until it's warm.

# Fried Oysters with Napa Cabbage Slaw and Cilantro Chutney

I am a big fan of oysters. Other than freshly shucked right out of the water, fried is my favorite way to eat these briny bivalves. This recipe is a great alternative to more traditional preparations. The mayonnaise-based slaw provides a creamy base and the cilantro chutney adds a flavorful acidic bite to cut the richness of both the oysters and the slaw.

The key to good fried oysters, and I bet you know where I'm headed with this, is to buy good oysters from a trusted source. The preshucked variety, usually sold in cup or pint amounts, are fine if you're confident your market is selling them briskly enough that they are fresh. A better alternative is to shuck them yourself or have your fishmonger shuck them for you. The other consideration is size. Oysters come in various sizes, depending on the variety. For fried oysters, you want to have slightly larger oysters than you might choose if you were eating them raw. If the oysters are too small, they will taste more like breading than oysters. Be sure to make the slaw and the chutney first, as cooking the oysters takes just a few minutes and cold fried oysters are not very tasty.

1. Soak the oysters in the buttermilk while you assemble the remaining ingredients.

2. Spread the panko in a shallow bowl and toss the soaked oysters in the panko, a few at a time, pressing the breading with your hands lightly around the oysters to make sure the coating adheres evenly. When the oysters are breaded, transfer them to a plate. Bread all the oysters before you start cooking.

3. Heat the oil in a large, heavy sauté pan over medium heat.

4. When the oil is shimmering but before it starts to smoke, carefully place as many breaded oysters in the pan as you can without crowding.

5. Cook for about 1 minute on each side or until the breading is golden brown.

*(Continued)*

**Yield: 4 servings**

36 oysters, shucked

1 cup buttermilk

3 to 4 cups panko bread crumbs

1 cup vegetable oil, plus more as needed

1 batch Napa Cabbage Slaw (recipe follows)

Cilantro Chutney (recipe follows)

6. Remove the oysters from the pan and place them on paper towels to drain.

7. Serve the oysters on a bed of the Napa Cabbage Slaw and drizzle some of the chutney around the plate.

## Napa Cabbage Slaw

**Yield: about 4 cups slaw**

2 pounds napa cabbage

1 cup chopped scallions

1½ cups mayonnaise

2 tablespoons soy sauce

2 teaspoons dry mustard

½ teaspoon freshly ground black pepper

1. Cut the cabbage into quarters lengthwise and cut out the core. Cut into ⅛-inch strips crosswise and put in a large bowl.

2. Add the scallions, mayonnaise, soy sauce, dry mustard, and pepper to the cabbage and mix thoroughly.

3. The slaw will keep for 3 to 4 days in the refrigerator.

## Cilantro Chutney

**Yield: 1 cup chutney**

2 cups coarsely chopped fresh cilantro (1 to 2 bunches)

1 to 2 serrano chilies, seeded

2 tablespoons finely chopped fresh ginger

1 cup chopped scallions (about 1 bunch)

1 teaspoon kosher salt

2 tablespoons freshly squeezed lime juice

¼ cup extra-virgin olive oil

1. Pulverize the cilantro, chilies, ginger, scallions, salt, and lime juice in a food processor or blender.

2. Slowly add the olive oil and process until the mixture resembles pesto. You may need to scrape down the sides of the machine a few times to ensure that all the ingredients are blended evenly. Store in an airtight container under refrigeration. The chutney will last 2 to 3 days.

## Salmon with Savoy Cabbage, Caramelized Pearl Onions, and Bacon

Northwesterners take their salmon very seriously. While I like Atlantic salmon and will cook and eat it happily, nothing compares to wild salmon. I was first introduced to this wonderfully rich, flavorful fish when I was 17, shortly after moving to the Northwest. My father would cook whole sides of salmon on the grill with nothing but butter, lemon, a few sprigs of dill, and salt and pepper. My father was a great and talented man, but cooking really wasn't his bag, and while it might sound like I'm about to bash his salmon-cooking skills, I'm not. This was his dish and he would nail it every time. He also would have loved this salmon recipe.

*(Continued)*

**Yield: 4 servings**

¼ cup plus 2 tablespoons olive oil, divided

¼ pound bacon, sliced into ½-inch pieces

2 cups red or white pearl onions, peeled

2 pounds savoy cabbage, cut into 1-inch pieces

4 teaspoons kosher salt, divided

½ teaspoon freshly ground black pepper

2 cups chicken stock, store-bought or homemade (page 253)

2 tablespoons unsalted butter

2 tablespoons chopped fresh rosemary

2 tablespoons chopped fresh parsley

4 (6-ounce) salmon portions, skinned (about 1½ pounds)

1. Preheat oven to 425°F.

2. Heat 2 tablespoons of the olive oil in an 8-quart saucepot over medium-low heat. Add the bacon and the pearl onions and cook for 10 to 15 minutes or until the bacon is crisp and the onions are browned and caramelized. Pull the pot from the heat, remove the bacon and onions, and set aside.

3. Return the pot to the burner over medium heat and add the cabbage. Season with 1 teaspoon kosher salt and the pepper and cook for about 5 minutes or until it begins to soften.

4. Add the chicken stock and cook for an additional 10 to 15 minutes. Scrape the pot with a spatula to release any tasty bacon and onion bits that might be lurking on the bottom. Add the butter and herbs and check the seasoning. The broth from the pot will be your sauce.

5. Rinse and dry the salmon portions under cold running water and pat dry with paper towels. Season both sides of the salmon portions with 1 tablespoon of the salt.

6. Heat the remaining ¼ cup of olive oil in a 10- to 12-inch, heavy, ovenproof sauté pan over medium-high heat.

7. When the oil is just about to smoke, carefully place the salmon portions, flesh side down, in the pan, making sure not to over-crowd the pan. To develop a nice golden crust, sear the fish for 3 to 5 minutes without shaking the pan or fiddling with the fish portions. Without flipping the fish, place the whole pan, uncovered, in your preheated oven and cook for an additional 5 minutes or until the fish is medium rare, or longer if you prefer medium. Alternatively, if your pan is not big enough to cook all the pieces at once, sear the fish in batches until you have a nice crust on one side, then transfer, seared side up, to a baking sheet and finish in the oven as described.

8. Place the cabbage and some of the liquid in the middle of the plate, place a piece of salmon on top of the cabbage, and sprinkle the pearl onions and bacon pieces around the plate.

## Panfried Softshell Crab over Cajun Coleslaw with Brown Butter Lemon Vinaigrette

I was in my early twenties before I had my first softshell crab. In fact, I'd never even heard of them until I was in culinary school and was offered a softshell crab po'boy for lunch. "What's a softshell crab?" I asked. It's a blue crab that is harvested during its molting cycle when the new shell is still soft and edible. "You eat the whole thing, shell and all?" Yes. "What? No way!" Yes way. Still a bit skeptical, I ordered the sandwich. Boom! Mind blown! New favorite thing ever! A few thousand softies later, they are still one of my favorite things.

In our recipe, the crispy crab and spicy slaw capture the essence of the po'boy, while the brown butter lemon vinaigrette and roasted pecans provide an elegant richness to the finished dish. Fresh, live

*(Continued)*

softshell crabs are available from late spring through the fall, depending on your region, but they also freeze fairly well and are consequently available frozen year-round. If you're buying fresh crabs, you or your fishmonger will need to clean them. Frozen crabs are sold cleaned. They come in various sizes; plan 2 per person unless they're huge.

**Yield: 4 servings**

8 softshell crabs, cleaned (see note)

1½ cups buttermilk

1 cup all-purpose flour

1 cup cornstarch

1 cup cornmeal

1 tablespoon kosher salt, plus more for sprinkling

1 teaspoon freshly ground black pepper, plus more for sprinkling

2 cups vegetable oil, for panfrying

1 batch Cajun Coleslaw (page 175)

1 cup chopped pecans, toasted

1 batch Brown Butter Lemon Vinaigrette (recipe follows)

1 cup chopped tomatoes

¼ cup chopped fresh parsley

¼ cup chopped scallions

1. Combine the cleaned crabs with the buttermilk in a medium bowl, making sure they are evenly coated. Let them soak while you're getting your breading and panfrying setup ready.

2. Combine the flour, cornstarch, cornmeal, and salt and pepper in a bowl or pan large enough to dredge the crabs.

3. While the oil is heating up, dredge the crabs in the flour mixture.

4. Carefully lift a crab out of the buttermilk and let it drain back into the bowl for a second, then place it in the breading mixture. Gently roll the crab around, making sure you coat it evenly and that you get some coating under the hood where the gills used to be. Place the coated crab on another plate and repeat until all the crabs are coated and ready to go.

5. When the oil is shimmering and just about to smoke, carefully add the crabs to the hot oil without crowding your pan. Fry the crabs a few at a time for 2 minutes on each side. Gently remove the crabs from the oil and place on a paper towel to drain and keep warm while you cook the remaining crabs. Season the hot crabs with a little more salt and pepper.

6. Place a mound of coleslaw in the center of each plate, stack a couple of crabs on top, and sprinkle the toasted pecans over the crabs and around the plate. Drizzle 3 to 4 tablespoons of the warm vinaigrette over the crabs and around the plate, and garnish with the chopped tomato, parsley, and scallions.

**NOTE:** Cleaning softshell crabs, or more accurately slaying and cleaning, is simple but not for the faint of heart. Some may, for various reasons, have a hard time with this part, so if you're squeamish, have your fishmonger clean them for you. If you want the freshest crabs possible or if you're a little ghoulish, here we go. Take a pair of scissors and cut off the face just behind the eyes. Carefully lift up each side of the top shell and, with your fingers, remove the bitter-tasting gills. OK, last step: Flip the crab over and remove the apron, which is the small flap toward the back of the crab opposite where the face used to be. Both male and female crabs have aprons, but the size and shape are different. Female crabs have a wider apron that spans most of the width of the crab, whereas the male apron is much thinner. That's it; you're done.

## Brown Butter Lemon Vinaigrette

This is a great all-purpose vinaigrette for fish and shellfish. We always have some around just in case we need a quick sauce. The lemon juice provides a sharp contrast to the rich, nutty flavor of the brown butter. The two main components will separate easily, so make sure you mix the vinaigrette thoroughly right before serving.

**Yield: 1½ cups vinaigrette**

2 cups (4 sticks) unsalted butter

⅓ cup freshly squeezed lemon juice

½ cup finely chopped shallots (3 to 4 shallots)

1 teaspoon kosher salt

½ teaspoon freshly ground black pepper

1. Heat the butter in a small saucepot over medium heat until the milk solids separate and fall to the bottom of the pan. Reduce the heat to low and continue to cook until the milk solids turn dark brown and the butter gives off a nutty aroma. You want the butter to be as dark as it can be without burning. This should take 20 to 30 minutes.

2. Remove from the heat and allow to cool for at least 30 minutes. Once the butter has cooled (see note), add the lemon juice and shallots and season with the salt and pepper.

**NOTE:** If you add the lemon juice to the hot butter, it will boil over and cause a big mess. If you make that mistake with the pot still on the burner and it foams over onto an open flame or electric burner, you could have a small grease fire, so be careful. Once the two parts are blended, you can reheat the sauce over low heat until it's warm.

## Prosciutto-Wrapped Cod with Vegetables Provençal

This is a light, simple, and delicious dish. The vegetables are available year-round but are at their best in the summer, when there is a large variety of summer squash in the market and the grape tomatoes are super sweet. The Vegetables Provençal also makes a lovely stand-alone, summery side dish.

Tell your butcher that you need long, thin slices of prosciutto with a little extra fat left on. The extra fat will disappear when you cook it, but it helps hold the prosciutto onto the fish.

**Yield: 4 servings**

4 (5- to 6-ounce) cod portions (about 1½ pounds)

¼ pound thinly sliced prosciutto

¼ cup olive oil, plus more if necessary

3 cups large-diced mixed summer squash in as many colors as you can find

1½ cups washed large-diced leek

6 garlic cloves, thinly sliced

1½ cups grape tomatoes

½ cup pitted Kalamata olives, cut in half

½ cup white wine

1 tablespoon unsalted butter

¼ cup torn fresh basil leaves

¼ cup chopped fresh parsley

1. Preheat oven to 425°F.

2. Rinse the cod portions under cold running water and pat them dry with paper towels. Wrap the prosciutto around the cod (see note).

3. Heat the olive oil in a large, heavy sauté pan over medium-high heat. When the oil is shimmering, add the wrapped cod portions and sauté for 3 to 4 minutes or until the prosciutto starts to brown. Cooking in batches, if necessary, to prevent crowding the pan.

4. Being careful not to rip the prosciutto when flipping the fish or removing it from the pan, turn the fish over and sauté the other side for 2 to 3 minutes, then transfer the browned cod portions to a baking sheet. Set the baking sheet aside.

5. In the same pan you used for the cod, sauté the squash, leek, and garlic over medium-heat for about 5 minutes. Add a little more olive oil, if necessary.

6. Add the tomatoes and olives and continue to cook for 2 minutes. Add the white wine and butter and cook for an additional 2 minutes. Remove from the heat, add the basil and parsley, and keep warm.

7. Place the baking sheet with the cod portions in the oven for 8 minutes. The prosciutto should be golden brown and the fish firm to the touch.

8. To serve, make a bed of the vegetables on each plate and place a cod portion on top.

**NOTE:** To wrap the cod, overlap 2 pieces of prosciutto with the fat bands on the outside to a width equal to the length of the cod pieces you're wrapping. Lay the two slightly overlapping prosciutto slices down on your work surface. Place a cod portion at one end and roll up the fish in the prosciutto. It's that simple.

## Halibut with Wilted Spinach, Roasted Shiitakes, and Mushroom Nage

This is a great dish for a dinner party. There are several steps, and preparing the stock takes several, albeit mostly unattended, hours. But with the exception of finishing the sauce and cooking the fish, everything can be done in advance.

Halibut is a flounderlike flatfish found in the both North Atlantic and North Pacific waters. Although the most common commercial size for these bottom-dwelling flatfish is 20 to 80 pounds, they can grow as large as 500 pounds. When I was cooking in Seattle, it often took two of us to carry a single halibut from the delivery truck into the kitchen. Uncooked, halibut is almost translucent. Cooked, the fish loses its glossy appearance and becomes snow white, flaky, and firm.

**Yield: 2 cups; 4 servings**

6 cups chicken stock, store-bought or homemade (page 253)

1½ pounds button mushrooms

1 carrot, chopped

1 onion, chopped

2 celery ribs, chopped

3 garlic cloves

2 bay leaves

½ teaspoon dried thyme

½ teaspoon dried rosemary

¼ cup (½ stick) unsalted butter

1 tablespoon fresh rosemary

1 tablespoon chopped fresh parsley

1 tablespoon unsalted butter

1 pound spinach, washed

½ teaspoon kosher salt

The earthy flavors of the wilted spinach and roasted shiitake mushrooms complement the mild briny sweetness of halibut. A nage is flavorful liquid that is traditionally used to poach fish or shellfish and is then enriched with cream or butter and used as a sauce. Here, we're not using it for poaching, but simply adding butter and herbs to the mushroom stock, resulting in a deeply flavorful, velvety, rich sauce.

## Mushroom Stock and Nage

1. Combine the chicken stock, vegetables, garlic, and dried herbs in a 4-quart saucepot and bring to boil.

2. Lower the heat to medium-low and simmer for about 2 hours or until the liquid has reduced by half.

3. Strain the liquid through a sieve or colander, discard the solids, and return the stock to the pot. Continue to reduce the strained stock over medium-low heat until you have about 2 cups.

4. You will finish the sauce with the butter and fresh herbs when your halibut is in the oven.

## Wilted Spinach

1. Place a wire rack on a baking sheet to drain the spinach once it is cooked.

2. Heat the butter in a 6-quart saucepot over medium-high heat. This might seem like a large pot for 1 pound of spinach, but if you use a smaller one, it will steam, not wilt.

3. Once the butter has stopped bubbling and has begun to brown, add all the spinach at once, season with the salt, and, using tongs or a spoon, immediately start stirring the spinach. You should expect the spinach to pop and crackle a bit as the moisture is released into the hot butter. Keep stirring the spinach until the leaves are just beginning to wilt, then quickly transfer it onto the wire rack to drain and cool. The wilting process will only take a few seconds.

*(Continued)*

4.  Allow the spinach to drain until it is cool. Place on an ovenproof dish to reheat when you're ready to assemble the dish.

## Shiitake Mushrooms

¼ cup olive oil

½ pound shiitake mushrooms, stemmed and halved (you can add the stems to the mushroom stock while it is reducing)

½ teaspoon salt

1 tablespoon unsalted butter

2 teaspoons chopped fresh oregano

2 teaspoons chopped fresh thyme

2 teaspoons chopped fresh sage

2 teaspoons chopped fresh parsley

1.  Heat the olive oil in a large sauté pan over high heat. The pan should be big enough that you can sear all the mushrooms without crowding the pan.

2.  When the oil is beginning to smoke, add the shiitakes, spreading them evenly around the pan. Try to resist the urge to shake the pan or move the mushrooms around too much at this point. Mushrooms are mostly water and act like little sponges. You don't want them to burn, but if you move them around too much they will release their water and you will not get the color we're looking for.

3.  When the mushrooms begin to brown, after about 2 to 3 minutes, stir in the butter and herbs. Cook for 1 minute more and transfer to the rack with the spinach. When they are cool, add them to the dish along with the spinach.

## Fish

4 (6-ounce) halibut portions, skin removed

2 teaspoons kosher salt

½ teaspoon freshly ground white pepper

6 tablespoons olive oil

1.  Preheat oven to 425°F.

2.  Rinse and thoroughly dry your halibut portions, then season the fish with the salt and pepper.

3.  Heat the olive oil in a heavy, ovenproof, 10- to 12-inch sauté pan over medium-high heat. When the oil is just beginning to smoke, gently place the halibut, flesh side down, in the hot pan. Sear the fish for 2 to 3 minutes on the stovetop and, without flipping the fish, place the whole pan in the oven to cook, uncovered, for an additional 4 to 5 minutes. Alternatively, if you don't have a pan big enough to cook all the pieces at once, don't worry. Just sear the fish in smaller batches for 3 to 4 minutes on one side, then transfer the

portions to a baking sheet, seared side up, and finish cooking in the oven for an additional 3 to 4 minutes.

4. When you put the fish in the oven, put the baking pan of spinach and shiitakes in the oven too so they can reheat.

5. Finish the sauce by bringing the stock to a boil. Add the butter 1 tablespoon at a time, stirring after each addition, and then add the fresh rosemary and parsley. Remove from the heat.

6. When the fish is cooked and the vegetables are hot, remove them from the oven and make a small pile of the wilted spinach in the center of each plate. Place the halibut portions, seared side up, on top of the spinach and distribute the roasted shiitakes around the plate. Give the sauce a final whisk and spoon over and around the fish.

## Frogs' Legs Sauce Piquant

### Frogs' legs:

24 pairs frogs' legs (about 2 pounds)

2 tablespoons kosher salt

2 teaspoons freshly ground black pepper

1 cup all-purpose flour

½ cup olive oil, plus more if needed

2 tablespoons chopped fresh parsley

Steamed white or brown rice, for serving

You don't see a whole lot of frogs' legs on menus up here in the Northeast. This is good news for the frog population but bad news for us, because they're delicious. If you're looking for something out of the norm for a dinner party, this is a great option. Take some odds on how long it takes for one of your guests to make the first Kermit joke. And when they ask, yes, it really does taste a lot like chicken. Keep this dish simple and serve with some white or brown rice. While I doubt any grocery store north of Louisiana or Mississippi will have frogs' legs, your butcher or fishmonger should be able to order them for you, or they are available online. If you really can't get past the frogs' legs, the sauce and method are equally delicious used with chicken, rabbit, fish, or pork.

**Yield: 4 to 6 servings**

## *Sauce piquant*

¼ cup (½ stick) unsalted butter

¼ cup all-purpose flour

2 cups chopped onions

½ cup seeded and chopped red bell pepper

½ cup seeded and chopped green bell pepper

½ cup chopped celery

2 tablespoons finely chopped garlic

1 teaspoon kosher salt

½ teaspoon freshly ground black pepper

1 cup white wine

1 cup chicken or shellfish stock, store-bought or homemade (pages 253 and 258)

1 (14-ounce) can diced tomatoes with juice

½ teaspoon cayenne pepper

½ teaspoon chili powder

½ teaspoon smoked paprika

2 tablespoons chopped fresh thyme

1. **Prepare the sauce:** Melt the butter in a heavy 10-inch sauté pan over medium heat. Whisk in the flour and cook for about 10 minutes or until the roux is medium brown, about the color of peanut butter.

2. Add the onion, peppers, celery, and garlic, season to taste with the kosher salt and black pepper, and cook for 10 minutes or until the vegetables begin to soften.

3. Pour in the white wine, stock, and tomatoes and bring the mixture to a simmer, stirring, to make sure the roux is well incorporated. Add the cayenne, chili powder, and smoked paprika.

4. Lower the heat to maintain a gentle simmer for 15 minutes while you prepare the frogs' legs.

5. **Prepare the frogs' legs:** Rinse the frogs' legs under running water, then drain in a colander and pat dry with paper towels. Spread them out in a single layer on a baking tray and season both sides with salt and pepper.

6. Spread the flour in a shallow dish. Dredge the frogs' legs in the flour, tapping off the excess.

7. Heat the olive oil in a large, heavy sauté pan over medium-high heat. When the oil is shimmering, sauté the frogs' legs in small batches, without crowding your pan, for 3 to 4 minutes on each side, or until they are fully cooked and golden brown. When the frogs' legs are cooked, transfer them to a plate lined with paper towels and keep warm.

8. Stir the thyme into the sauce just before serving. Spoon the sauce onto a serving platter and arrange the frogs' legs on the sauce, then spoon a little more sauce over the frogs' legs. Sprinkle the parsley over the top and serve with steamed white or brown rice.

# Peel-and-Eat Shrimp

We put peel-and-eat shrimp on the menu a few years ago, when we were looking for something to take the place of the Savory BBQ Shrimp (page 49) for the summer. I wanted something that was fun to share, and I'll admit it, something that was going to be easy to execute during the busy summer. We had served peel-and-eat shrimp at our annual crawfish festival as an alternative for those folks who didn't want to deal with the carnage of dismembering crawfish. It has a lot of the same appeal: everyone sitting round the table, getting their hands a little dirty, sucking the buttery spices off their fingers, and having a great time doing it. It's just easier and the work-to-reward ratio is considerably better.

When there is only one ingredient in a dish, you need to make sure it's the best, and fortunately for us, some of the best shrimp in the world comes right through our back door in the Gulf of Mexico. If that seems too far, realize that almost any other shrimp is going to be coming from halfway around the world. Ask your fishmonger for wild gulf shrimp. You will see and taste the difference. The Mississippi Salsa goes great with the shrimp.

*(Continued)*

**Yield: 4 servings**

6 quarts water

¼ cup plus 1 tablespoon Old Bay Seasoning, divided

¼ cup plus 1 tablespoon Hattie's Crawfish/Shrimp Boil (page 101) or commercial crab/shrimp boil, divided

4 bay leaves

1 garlic bulb, cut in half

Juice of 2 lemons

2 pounds wild gulf shrimp (21/25 or 16/20 per pound)

2 tablespoons unsalted butter

1 batch Mississippi Salsa (recipe follows)

1. Combine the water, ¼ cup Old Bay, ¼ cup crawfish/shrimp boil, bay leaves, garlic, and lemon juice in an 8-quart stockpot and bring to a boil over high heat. Lower the heat and simmer for 15 minutes so the flavor of the boil will develop and blend.

2. Rinse the shrimp under cold running water and drain in a colander.

3. Combine the butter and the reserved tablespoons of the Old Bay and crawfish/shrimp boil in a bowl large enough to hold and toss the shrimp when they've finished cooking.

4. Increase the heat under the pot to resume a boil. Pour all the shrimp into the pot at the same time. The cold shrimp will immediately stop the liquid from boiling. Give the shrimp a stir and keep the heat on high until the liquid starts to simmer again, then adjust the heat to maintain a lazy bubble just below a simmer. Cook for a total of 4 to 5 minutes from the time you put the shrimp in the pot.

5. Transfer the shrimp to a colander and allow to drain and steam for 2 minutes.

6. Slide the hot shrimp into the bowl with the butter mixture and toss until the butter has melted and the seasonings are evenly distributed.

7. Turn out the shrimp onto a platter, grab some napkins and a beer, and dig in.

**Yield: about 1¼ cups salsa**

1 cup ketchup or chili sauce

¼ cup prepared horseradish

2 teaspoons freshly squeezed lemon juice

½ teaspoon Worcestershire sauce

½ teaspoon hot sauce

¼ teaspoon freshly ground black pepper

# Mississippi Salsa

Mississippi Salsa, a.k.a. cocktail sauce, is the classic accompaniment to shrimp or crab cocktail. This version has a sharp horseradish kick and takes only seconds to make.

1. Blend all the ingredients together in a small bowl.

2. Store refrigerated in an airtight container for up to 2 weeks.

## Monkfish with Clams and Chorizo

A whole monkfish is a crazy-looking beast. Almost all head, with a broad row of sharp teeth and winglike pectoral fins, it looks more like a sea monster than something you would want to eat. At the Pike Place Market in Seattle, one of the fishmongers used to play a clever trick on customers. He would lay a whole monkfish on the ice and prop open its wide mouth with a stick to display all its sharp teeth. The stick was attached to fishing line that ran back through the ice. When an unsuspecting victim, usually a tourist, got close enough, the guy behind the counter would yank the stick, making the fish jump and the mouth close, giving the appearance that the fish was still very much alive. Fun, for sure, but I doubt it increased monkfish sales.

Regardless of appearance, it's a great eating fish. Its firm, slightly sweet flesh is dense and meaty and is often compared in texture to lobster. Because of its density, monkfish is a great choice for someone who

*(Continued)*

isn't too confident cooking fish. Unlike a lot of other fish that become dry if overcooked, the density of monkfish provides a little moisture insurance. Similar to meat, it benefits from a couple minutes of resting time between cooking and serving.

This recipe is a little long, but it's not complicated. Even though you will use three pans, there is a logical progression of steps. It will be helpful to have all your ingredients prepped and ready to go before you start cooking.

**Yield: 4 servings**

4 new potatoes (2 to 3 inches in diameter)

6 garlic cloves, peeled

2 bay leaves

1 teaspoon dried rosemary

1 teaspoon dried thyme

1 tablespoon kosher salt

## Potatoes

1. Combine the potatoes, garlic, bay leaves, rosemary, thyme, and salt into a small saucepot and cover with cold water by at least an inch. Bring the potatoes to a boil and reduce the heat to maintain a low simmer.

2. Cook the potatoes for about 15 minutes or until you can insert a skewer or paring knife through the center of the potato with only slight resistance. Pull the pot off the heat and allow the potatoes to cool in the water while you prepare the rest of the dish.

¼ cup olive oil

½ pound chorizo sausage, sliced

2 cups thinly sliced onions

2 red bell peppers, seeded and thinly sliced

5 garlic cloves, thinly sliced

1 teaspoon Spanish paprika

24 littleneck clams, rinsed

2 cups clam juice, or fish or chicken stock, store-bought or homemade (pages 257 and 253)

1 tablespoon chopped fresh rosemary

1 tablespoon chopped fresh thyme

1 tablespoon chopped fresh sage

## Chorizo and Clams

1. Preheat oven to 425°F. Choose a large, heavy sauté pan or saucepot that has a lid.

2. Heat the olive oil in the pan over medium-high heat. When the oil is shimmering, add the chorizo and brown the sausage for 5 minutes or until evenly browned.

3. Add the onions, bell peppers, garlic, and paprika to the chorizo and continue to cook over medium heat until the vegetables are just starting to soften and lose their shape, about 5 minutes.

4. Add the clams and the clam juice or stock and cover the pan. Increase the heat to medium-high and cook until all the clams have opened. This should take about 10 minutes. Give the clams a stir a couple of times during this process to help them open and ensure

that the mixture cooks evenly. Once the clams open, add the rosemary, thyme, and sage to the pot and remove from the heat. Remove and discard any clams that haven't opened. Return the lid to the pot.

## Monkfish

1. Choose a heavy, ovenproof pan large enough to accommodate the fish portions with some room to spare. If you crowd the fish, it will be more difficult to sear and harder to achieve a nice brown color.

2. Rinse the monkfish under cold running water and pat dry with paper towels. Season with the salt and white pepper.

3. Heat the olive oil until it begins to smoke. Carefully place the fish portions in the pan so they aren't touching. Try to resist the urge to shake the pan or move the fish at this point. The goal here is to achieve a rich golden crust; moving the fish or shaking the pan releases moisture and hinders the searing process.

4. Continue to cook the fish on medium-high heat for 3 to 4 minutes. Then, without turning the fish, put the pan in a preheated 425°F oven. Cook the fish in the oven, uncovered, for an additional 8 to 10 minutes.

5. Remove the pan from the oven and carefully turn the fish so that the seared side faces up. Allow the fish to rest while you build the plate.

6. Remove the potatoes with a slotted spoon, slice into ¼-inch slices, and place in a small pile in the center of the individual plates or bowls you will use to serve the dish. With a spoon or tongs, pile some of the peppers and the sausage mixture on top of the potatoes. Place a fish portion on top and surround the fish with a few of the clams and some broth.

7. Sprinkle each plate with the fresh parsley and serve with some crusty bread to soak up the broth.

4 (6- to 7-ounce) portions cleaned monkfish portions (about 2 pounds; see note)

1 tablespoon kosher salt

1 teaspoon freshly ground white pepper

½ cup olive oil

2 tablespoons chopped fresh parsley

Crusty bread, for serving

**NOTE:** Ask your fishmonger to make sure the monkfish is cleaned. Uncleaned monkfish has a thin, silvery-blue membrane surrounding the meat. The membrane is not palatable. You can remove it yourself with a sharp boning knife or paring knife, but it really should come already cleaned.

earth and air

## Grilled Maple-Cured Pork Tenderloin

Pork has been on a steady comeback in restaurants for the past few years. From whole roasted pigs to pork belly to pork shanks, it is increasingly becoming a more attractive menu option for chefs. This is due in part to its relatively low cost when compared to other meat options, such as beef, lamb, or game, and its versatility. For my money, there is really no other animal that gives the chef as many options for preparation as the pig. Depending on the cut, pork can stand on its own with little more than salt and pepper or benefit from a little tinkering, usually in the form of rubs, marinades, and brines. Pork tenderloin is one of those cuts that can do both equally well. This brine will give the tenderloin just a touch of sweetness, while the spices provide savory structure to keep everything in balance. You can use the brine on any cut of pork, but the amount of time the meat is left in the brine will vary depending on the cut and size. For pork tenderloin, 24 hours is about right.

**Yield: 4 to 6 servings**

## *Apple cider brine:*

2 cups apple cider

2 cups water

¼ cup pure maple syrup

2 tablespoons molasses

½ cup light brown sugar

¼ cup kosher salt

½ teaspoon freshly ground black pepper

½ teaspoon ground ginger

½ teaspoon dry mustard

¼ teaspoon ground allspice

3 bay leaves

2 pork tenderloins, trimmed (about 2 pounds)

¼ cup olive oil

1. **Prepare the brine:** In a medium bowl, combine the apple cider, water, maple syrup, molasses, brown sugar, salt, spices, and bay leaves, whisking until the sugar and salt have dissolved.

2. Place the pork in a gallon-size resealable plastic bag or container so that the entire surface of each pork tenderloin is covered with the brine. Leave the tenderloins in the brine, refrigerated, for at least 12 to 24 hours.

3. Fire up your grill to a high temperature. If your grill has a temperature gauge, 450° to 500°F is what you want.

4. Remove the pork from the brine, pat dry with paper towels, and rub with the olive oil.

5. Grill over direct heat until all sides of the tenderloin are browned with a little char and the internal temperature reads 140° to 145°F. This should take about 20 minutes, depending on the temperature of your grill. Allow to rest for 5 minutes before serving.

# Pot Roast

Good ol' pot roast. There are few dishes as significant to the repertoire of American classics as pot roast. In past generations, families never went more than a week or two without having this iconic dish. Now, I would bet that for most American families, it's not even in the rotation. In fact, based on my experience at the restaurant, most people under the age of 50 either can't remember the last time they had pot roast or, based on the look I get, don't know exactly what it is.

Cooking pot roast has almost been narrowed to a culinary school exercise for fledgling chefs learning the fine art of braising. Even these would-be supporters quickly drop the dish for sexier versions of braised meats, such as short ribs or osso buco. But there is a reason it's taught in culinary school. A well-executed, succulent pot roast demonstrates that the cook has control over a number of cooking techniques, knows how they work in concert, and possesses the patience and skill to coax flavor and texture from an inexpensive and tough piece of meat.

Give it a try. Much of the work is passive, and the rewards far out-weigh the effort. You will also be doing your part to nurture America's understanding of its own culinary heritage. Even with the recent popularity of the farm-to-table and locavore movements, America is still just beginning to explore and understand the cultural connection to its food. Pot roast is a delicious, rich, soul-satisfying dish that will make you and anyone you share it with happy. All right, I'm done. I'll get off my soapbox now.

I want to give you fair warning that, like most braised dishes, pot roast is better if you let it sit for a day. Not only will the texture of the meat be better, but it is much easier to remove the fat that cooks out of the chuck once it has cooled and risen to the top. The pan you choose should be wide enough that the chuck will fit comfortably while you're searing it, but deep enough so that when you add your liquids they will come one-half to two-thirds up the side of the chuck. Ideally you want to use the same pan throughout the cooking process so no flavor is lost.

*(Continued)*

**Yield: 8 to 10 servings**

1 (4- to 5-pound) well-marbled beef chuck roast

¼ cup kosher salt

1 tablespoon freshly ground black pepper

½ cup all-purpose flour

¾ cup vegetable oil, divided

2 onions, peeled and chopped

2 carrots, peeled and cut into 1-inch pieces

2 celery ribs, cut into 1-inch pieces

5 garlic cloves, peeled

3 ounces tomato paste

2 cups red wine

3 sprigs fresh rosemary

3 sprigs fresh sage

¼ bunch fresh thyme (about 8 sprigs)

12 cups veal or chicken stock, store-bought or homemade (pages 254 and 253)

1. Rinse the chuck under cold running water and pat dry with a paper towel. Trim off any silver skin and have ready several feet of butcher's twine. Tie the chuck so that it will stay together and cook evenly. Depending on the shape of your roast, one or two loops in each direction should be sufficient. Season the trimmed and tied chuck with the salt and pepper and dust with the flour.

2. Preheat oven to 350°F. Heat ½ cup of the oil in a large Dutch oven or heavy stockpot over high heat. When the oil starts to smoke, carefully add the chuck and sear it until it turns dark brown on all sides. Depending on your stove, it could take up to 15 to 20 minutes to develop the deep, rich brown we're looking for. A great deal of the flavor of the final dish is developed in this stage and the next two, so take your time and adjust the heat as needed.

3. Once the chuck is a deep, dark brown, remove the pan from the heat, carefully remove the chuck, and set it aside. Discard the oil from the pan and add the remaining ¼ cup of fresh oil. Return the pan to medium-high heat and add the onions, carrots, and celery, stirring from time to time until they are turning golden brown, about 10 minutes. Lower the heat to medium and add the garlic and the tomato paste. Continue to cook, stirring frequently, for another 2 to 3 minutes.

4. Pour the red wine into the pan and gently scrape the bottom and sides of the pan to release any drippings that have developed. These crusty drippings are called the fond and it's where the flavor is. When the wine has reduced by half, put the chuck back in the pot along with any juices that might have accumulated and add the herbs.

5. Pour enough stock into the pan to come one-half to two-thirds up the side of the chuck. Bring the braising liquid to simmer over medium heat and place the pot in the oven. Braise the beef, uncovered, for about 4 hours, turning every hour or so to submerge the meat that was exposed. Add more stock as needed to keep the chuck covered with liquid by one-half to two-thirds.

6. When the pot roast is done, it should be soft, fork-tender, and pull apart easily. Remove from the oven and discard the vegetables and herbs.

7. Now you have a choice. If you're going to serve it another day, allow the roast to cool slightly, then put the whole pot in the refrigerator. When you are ready to reheat the roast, remove the fat that will have risen to the top. Remove the strings and heat gently in the braising liquid.

8. If you're going to serve the roast immediately, carefully transfer it to a serving dish, remove the strings, and cover to keep warm.

9. Set the pot over medium-low heat and bring the braising liquid to a gentle simmer. Slide the pot off to one side of the burner. This will start a circular convection of the braising liquid and push the fat and any impurities to the top and side of the pot so you can remove them with a spoon or ladle.

10. Slice or break the pot roast into serving-size pieces. Pour the braising liquid over and around the pot roast and serve.

**NOTE:** Pot roast is often served with a variety of roasted root vegetables but is also delicious served on a bed of creamy grits or smashed potatoes.

## Andouille and Pimento Cheese Sliders

Like most people, I love a good burger. And, as much as I hate to concede defeat, America's love affair with burgers may be stronger than its love for fried chicken. *Slider* is really just a cute name for a small burger, and ours are equally good in a small or large format. The onion-spiked creaminess of the pimento cheese blends beautifully with the smokiness of the burger. It also provides an excellent opportunity to make a batch of pimento cheese and, in a pleasant way, force it on your friends and family. Pair the sliders or burgers with toasted brioche or potato rolls.

**Yield: about 12 sliders or 6 burgers**

1½ pounds ground beef (see note)

¾ pound finely chopped andouille sausage

2 tablespoons kosher salt

2 teaspoons freshly ground black pepper

¼ cup olive oil

12 brioche or potato rolls

2 tablespoons unsalted butter, melted

1 batch Pimento Cheese (page 62)

1. Place the ground beef in a medium-size bowl. Sprinkle the chopped sausage over the beef and season with the salt and pepper. Gently combine and form into patties. The size is really up to you. Two to 3 ounces is about right for a slider or 6 to 8 ounces for a traditional burger.

2. Preheat a large, heavy pan over medium-high heat and add the olive oil. Sear the burgers for 2 to 3 minutes on each side for rare to medium rare, or longer for medium and beyond. Cooking times also will vary depending on the size of patty. Alternatively, you could grill these, if you wish.

3. Butter the rolls with the melted butter and toast in the oven or on the grill.

4. Top the sliders with a generous dollop of Pimento Cheese.

**NOTE:** There is a lot of chatter about what makes one burger better than the next, and every burger restaurant from Red Robin to Shake Shack has its own proprietary blend of ground beef that's better than the next guy's. What's the takeaway? Not all ground beef is the same. Here are a couple of guidelines: First, use 80/20 ground beef. If the ground beef is too lean, your burger is likely to be dry. Second, choose a blend that has a good percentage of more flavorful cuts, such as chuck or brisket.

# Blackened Skirt Steak with Crispy Blue Cheese Grit Cakes and Smoked Tomato Butter

For many people, *blackened* is the first thing that comes to mind when they think of New Orleans or Cajun cuisine. This technique, popularized by the great chef Paul Prudhomme in the 1980s, is a great way to build spicy depth of flavor into almost any piece of meat, poultry, or fish that can hold up to the intense cooking method. Skirt steak works well because it is relatively thin, has a nice amount of marbling, and has a lot of flavor.

It may come as a surprise, but the technique of blackening does not mean burnt. Dark and a little charred maybe, but not burnt. What it means is coating your meat or fish thinly with room-temperature butter, dusting it liberally with Cajun or blackening spice, and searing it in a screaming-hot cast-iron pan. Depending on the thickness of the meat and the desired level of doneness, you might need to finish the cooking in the oven. We serve the steak with smoked tomato butter, which pivots nicely off the spicy char crust and blue cheese grit cakes.

This recipe is easy if all the components are prepared ahead, but the grit cakes, in particular, should be started a day before you plan to serve the dish. You may decide plain creamy grits are just fine, and you'd be right!

Also plenty of good blackening spice mixtures are available commercially. I've provided our Hattie's Hot Rub recipe in the event you choose to make your own.

**Yield: 4 servings**

2 pounds skirt steak

¼ cup (½ stick) unsalted butter at room temperature

¼ to ½ cup blackening spice, such as Hattie's Hot Rub (recipe follows)

1. Coat the skirt steak on both sides with the butter, dust heavily with the blackening spice, and let it sit until the oven and pan are hot.

2. Preheat oven to 425°F if you think you are going to need it (depending on how well done you prefer your steak), and preheat a cast-iron pan on the stove over high heat.

3. Place the buttered and spiced skirt steak in the hot, dry pan. Cook for about 2 minutes on each side. Finish in the oven, if necessary.

*(Continued)*

**Yield: ½ cup butter**

½ cup (1 stick) unsalted butter at room temperature

1 tablespoon tomato powder or 2 tablespoons sun-dried tomato paste

1 teaspoon liquid smoke

1 teaspoon kosher salt

¼ teaspoon freshly ground black pepper

**Yield: 4 grit cakes, about 2 x 2½ inches**

4 cups milk

2 bay leaves

1½ cups uncooked grits

2 teaspoons kosher salt

½ teaspoon freshly ground black pepper

6 ounces blue cheese

2 tablespoons olive oil

¼ cup all-purpose flour

# Smoked Tomato Butter

In a small bowl, combine all the ingredients. Butter the skirt steak before serving. The butter will keep for weeks in the refrigerator or months in the freezer.

# Blue Cheese Grit Cakes

Making grit cakes is very similar in process to the Basic Grits recipe (page 173), the major differences being the ratio of liquid to grits and the cooking time. You will need to dial back the heat a little and watch that the grits don't scorch. They are going to be a lot stiffer and gummier than the creamy grits, but you only need to cook them for about 10 minutes. Resist the urge to add liquid. They need to be on the dry side so that when they are cold they can be cut and fried without falling apart. The other key is to make the grits at least a day before you want to use them. They need time to set up so you can cut and cook them.

1.  Choose an appropriate dish for cooling and molding the grit cakes. An 8-inch cast-iron pan or an 8 x 8 x 2-inch baking dish works well. Unless the mold you choose has a nonstick coating, you will want to lightly coat it with pan spray or rub it with a little butter.

2.  In a 4-quart saucepot, bring the milk and the bay leaves to a boil over medium-high heat.

3.  Add the grits and reduce the heat to low. Stir constantly until the mixture begins to simmer. Very quickly the grits will go from creamy to stiff, but that is what we're looking for. Continue to cook for about 10 minutes, stirring frequently.

4.  Remove the bay leaves, add the salt and pepper, fold in the blue cheese, and scoop the grits into your prepared dish.

5.  With the back of a spoon or rubber spatula, spread the grits evenly, pressing into the corners to make sure there are no air pockets. Cover loosely with a piece of wax paper and allow them to cool on the counter for about 30 minutes before chilling in the refrigerator overnight.

**Yield: ½ cup hot rub**

2 tablespoons paprika

1 tablespoon smoked paprika

1 tablespoon freshly ground black pepper

1 tablespoon kosher salt

1 tablespoon garlic powder

1 tablespoon onion powder

1 tablespoon dried oregano leaves

1 tablespoon dried thyme leaves

1 teaspoon cayenne pepper

6. Unmold the grits onto the counter or cutting board and cut into your desired shapes. There are no rules on size or shape, so experiment. You can use a knife or cookie cutters.

7. Preheat a large, nonstick or cast-iron pan over medium heat and heat the oil. Dust the grit cakes with flour and sauté for 3 to 4 minutes on each side or until they are crispy and golden.

## Hattie's Hot Rub

Combine all the ingredients and store in an airtight container. The rub will keep for months.

# Warm Chicken, Bacon, and Arugula Salad

Let's say hypothetically that you roasted a chicken but didn't eat it all, and now you have some leftovers that, with a little fluffing, could be turned into a meal. This warm chicken salad might be just what you're looking for. We offer this on both the brunch and dinner menus because it appeals to diners who are in the mood for something on the lighter side, but still desire something tasty and full flavored. Dressing the arugula with the warm vinaigrette will wilt the greens just slightly and warm everything up enough to make the salad seem more substantial. Of course, you can make this salad with freshly cooked skinless chicken breasts or thighs if you don't have any leftovers.

**Yield: 2 servings**

4 slices bacon, cut into ½-inch pieces

8 ounces cooked chicken, cut into ½-inch pieces or shredded

1 batch Lemon Maple Vinaigrette (recipe follows)

5 ounces baby arugula

½ cup pecans, toasted

½ cup cherry or grape tomatoes, halved

1. Preheat an 8-inch sauté pan over medium-low heat and brown the bacon. When the bacon is browned and crispy, remove from the pan and drain on a paper towel.

2. Drain the bacon drippings and add the cooked chicken and vinaigrette to the pan. Warm over low heat for 2 to 3 minutes or until the chicken has warmed through and the vinaigrette is just starting to bubble.

3. Put the arugula in a medium-size to large bowl. Pour the warm vinaigrette mixture over the greens and toss to combine and slightly wilt the greens.

4. Divide the salad between two plates and garnish with the toasted pecans and tomatoes.

## Lemon Maple Vinaigrette

Combine the lemon juice and maple syrup in a small bowl. Whisk in the oil and season with salt and pepper.

**Yield: about ½ cup**

2 tablespoons freshly squeezed lemon juice

1 tablespoon pure maple syrup

¼ cup extra-virgin olive oil

Pinch of salt

Pinch of freshly ground black pepper

# Chicken-Fried Steak

Over the years I ran chicken-fried steak with smashed potatoes as a dinner special, and it always sold out. When we decided to start serving brunch, I knew I had the right spot to put chicken-fried steak on the menu for good. For brunch we serve it with gravy, two eggs any style, hash browns, and toast. It's restorative, rib-sticking comfort food regardless of when you eat it, and you can call the eggs a garnish if it makes you feel less guilty. You're going to use the three-stage breading process, with the only variation being that, after dipping the steaks into the egg wash, you're going to dredge them back into the flour instead of some other type of breading.

**Yield: 4 to 6 servings**

2 pounds cube steak

1 tablespoon kosher salt

1 teaspoon freshly ground black pepper

1 cup plus 3 tablespoons all-purpose flour, divided

3 large eggs, beaten

½ cup vegetable oil, plus more as needed

3 tablespoons unsalted butter

1½ cups chicken stock, store-bought or homemade (page 253)

½ cup milk

4–12 eggs

2 tablespoons chopped scallions

2 tablespoons chopped fresh parsley

1. Preheat oven to 200°F and set a wire cooling rack on a baking tray to keep the steaks warm while you make the gravy.

2. Season the steaks with the salt and pepper. Put 1 cup of the flour and the eggs in separate shallow bowls.

3. Dredge each steak in the flour until it is completely covered. Shake off the excess flour and then submerge the floured steak into the eggs, covering completely. Remove the steak from the eggs, redredge in the flour, and set aside. Bread all the steak before you start cooking.

4. Preheat a large, heavy sauté pan over medium-high heat and add the oil. There should be enough oil to completely cover the bottom of the pan, and you will need to add more oil as you cook the steaks.

5. When the oil is hot and shimmering, add as many steaks as you can without crowding the pan and cook for 3 minutes on each side, until they are golden brown. Transfer the steaks to the cooling rack and keep warm in the oven. Repeat this process until all the steaks have been cooked.

6. Pour off the cooking oil and wipe out the pan.

*(Continued)*

7. Return the pan to the burner and melt 3 tablespoons of butter over low heat. Add the remaining 3 tablespoons of flour and cook for 2 to 3 minutes while whisking. Be sure that the roux does not turn brown.

8. Add the chicken stock and milk to the roux. Increase the heat to medium-low and continue to whisk until the mixture comes to a simmer and begins to thicken. Cook at a low simmer for 5 minutes to cook out any floury taste. Check the seasoning of the gravy and adjust with salt and pepper.

9. Arrange the steaks on a plate, cover with the gravy, top with 1 to 2 eggs per person cooked the way you like them, and garnish with the scallions and parsley.

## Ribs Without a Smoker

I'm not going to argue that properly smoked pork ribs aren't superior in almost every way to those that have not been smoked, but I am going to tell you that you can make very good ribs in your oven. Now I love BBQ and come from a family that takes its BBQ as seriously as it does its pimento cheese. I want to be clear that by proposing this oven method I mean no disrespect to those dedicated to the gospel of BBQ and the search for smoky nirvana. This is for all those BBQ lovers stuck in small apartments in big cities or in some other situation where cranking up the smoker or grill for six hours is just not possible. Much of the process is the same. We will rub the ribs, let them rest overnight, cook them slowly just shy of falling off the bone, and then glaze them with tangy BBQ sauce to finish them off. We're just going to do it in the relative comfort of your kitchen. Do yourself a favor while you're at the

*(Continued)*

store buying the ribs and grab a large, disposable aluminum roasting pan or chafing dish that is at least 4 inches deep. They're cheap and you can use them for both seasoning and cooking the ribs. They will also make short work of the cleanup after the ribs are cooked.

This method is great if you want to have ribs for a party and have all the work done in advance. You can fully cook the ribs a day or two before your party and glaze them just before serving.

**NOTE:** This method works equally well for cooking a pork shoulder or pork butt for pulled pork BBQ. The cooking time will vary with the size of the roast, but figure about an hour per pound at 300°F. Do not try to glaze the pork butt in the oven. Add your BBQ sauce once the pork is cooked and pulled.

**Yield: 4 to 6 servings**

4 racks St. Louis–style pork spare ribs (about 2½ pounds each)

1 batch Dry Rub (recipe follows)

About 1 pint (16 ounces) of your favorite BBQ sauce, for glazing

1. Rinse the ribs under cold running water. Allow the excess water to run off the racks and place the ribs in your disposable pan.

2. Generously sprinkle the Dry Rub on both sides of the ribs and massage into the meat.

3. Cover with plastic wrap and place in the refrigerator for at least 4 to 5 hours, or for as long as 2 days.

4. Preheat oven to 275° to 300°F and set oven rack so the ribs will be in the center of your oven.

5. Remove the plastic wrap and overlap the ribs so they are evenly spaced and touching as little as possible. Cover and seal the pan tightly with aluminum foil and place in the oven. Set your timer for 4 hours and walk away. This is one of the best parts about cooking ribs in the oven. The ribs are going to take roughly 4 hours, and due to the lack of fire and smoke and the low temperature of the oven, you do not need to constantly monitor their progress.

6. After 4 hours, take a peek. Give the ribs a wiggle and gently try to pull two of the bones apart to check their texture. You want them to be tender and have some give, but they should not be mushy or soft. If you don't think they're quite done, re-cover the pan and place it back in the oven for another 30 minutes. Keep in mind that whether you eat them the same day or a few days later, they are

going to get another 45 minutes of cooking time when you glaze them, so factor that into your decision.

7. If you're going to serve the ribs on another day, let them rest on the counter until they are cool enough to handle. Then store them, covered, in the refrigerator.

8. To glaze the ribs, increase the oven temperature to 350°F. Brush a layer of your favorite BBQ sauce on the ribs and place the pan back in the oven. If your BBQ sauce is on the thicker side, you might want to thin it out with a little cider vinegar or water. The goal is to build up a patina of BBQ sauce over time, allowing each layer to caramelize slightly before adding the next layer.

9. Baste the ribs every 15 minutes or so for about an hour. When the ribs are glazed and luscious, arrange them on a platter with your favorite sides, maybe some Creole baked beans and cucumber salad.

## Dry Rub

**Yield: about 2½ cups dry rub**

1 cup light or dark brown sugar

½ cup kosher salt

¼ cup chili powder

¼ cup smoked paprika

2 tablespoons onion powder

2 tablespoons garlic salt

1 tablespoon freshly ground black pepper

1 tablespoon dry mustard

1 tablespoon Old Bay Seasoning

1 tablespoon dried rosemary

1 tablespoon dried thyme

Combine all the ingredients in a small bowl and mix thoroughly. The rub will keep indefinitely in an airtight container.

## Hattie's Meat Loaf

Meat loaf, while not indigenous to the South, is a quintessential American comfort food. Over the years, we typically have served our meat loaf at catering events or as a special, but due to customer requests we have recently added it to the regular menu. I prefer meat loaf made with a combination of beef, pork, and veal, which produces a juicer meat loaf with a finer texture and more balanced flavor profile than beef alone. The right binder is also important. I like crushed saltines or Ritz crackers. I find that they provide the right absorption level while remaining neutral in flavor. Many recipes suggest wrapping meat loaf in bacon. This can look great, but if flavor is your goal I would encourage you to take another approach. In this recipe we chop bacon into small pieces and mix it in with the other meats. I find that the bacon and its fat perform their function better from the

## Meat loaf:

**Yield: 6 to 8 servings**

1 pound ground beef, preferably chuck

½ pound ground pork

½ pound ground veal

½ pound finely chopped bacon

½ cup finely chopped onion

¼ cup finely chopped celery

¼ cup finely chopped carrot

2 tablespoons finely chopped garlic

½ cup milk or plain yogurt

3 large eggs, beaten

1 tablespoon Worcestershire sauce

1 tablespoon Hattie's Hot Sauce or other Louisiana-style hot sauce

1 teaspoon Dijon mustard

1 tablespoon kosher salt

2 teaspoons freshly ground pepper

¼ cup chopped fresh parsley

1 tablespoon chopped fresh thyme

1 tablespoon chopped fresh rosemary

1 cup crushed saltines or Ritz crackers

## Finishing glaze:

**Yield: 1 cup**

½ cup ketchup or chili sauce

¼ cup pepper jelly

¼ cup packed light brown sugar

6 tablespoons cider vinegar

inside. In keeping with my philosophy of building flavor into a dish, the yogurt is a nice alternative to the milk because it adds a little tang.

1. Preheat oven to 350°F.

2. Combine the beef, pork, veal, bacon, onion, celery, carrot, and garlic in a large bowl (see note).

3. Whisk together the milk, eggs, Worcestershire, hot sauce, mustard, and salt and pepper in a medium bowl.

4. Pour the milk mixture over the meat mixture and blend together until the liquid has been fully incorporated into the meat.

5. Sprinkle the fresh herbs and cracker crumbs over the meat and stir together until evenly distributed.

6. Turn out the mixture onto a rimmed baking sheet and shape into a roughly 9 x 4-inch loaf.

7. **Prepare the finishing glaze:** Combine all the ingredients in a small saucepan and bring to a simmer over medium-low heat. Once the sugar has dissolved and all the ingredients are combined, remove from the heat and set aside.

8. Bake for about 2 hours or until the internal temperature reads 160°F. After the first hour, baste the meat loaf with the glaze every 20 minutes to build up a thick patina of caramelized glaze. Allow the meat loaf to rest for 20 minutes before serving.

**NOTE:** You can use a wooden spoon or rubber spatula to mix all the ingredients if you wish but your hands are really the most efficient tools for this job.

## Jerk Chicken with Tropical Fruit Salsa and Scallion Aioli

Here's a reasonable question: Why does a restaurant that sells 50 percent fried chicken need another chicken dish on the menu? The answer is that, despite the overwhelming odds, there are always people who are in the mood for chicken but don't want their chicken fried. Out of all the nonfried chicken dishes we have tried, and there have been many over the years, it's the jerk chicken that has been the most popular. The jerk paste is intensely spiced and hot, but it's a balanced, fruity hot, not just whack-you-over-the-head hot. You can adjust the amount of jerk paste you rub on the chicken to suit your heat tolerance. The scallion aioli and the fruit salsa will also temper the heat. As with most marinated meat dishes, the chicken will be better if you coat it with the jerk paste at least a few hours, and up to a couple days, in advance.

**Yield: 1 cup jerk paste**

1 cup coarsely chopped onion

½ cup coarsely chopped scallions

3 garlic cloves, peeled

1 tablespoon chopped fresh ginger

2 habanero chilies or Scotch bonnet peppers, stemmed and seeded (see note)

1 serrano chili, stemmed and seeded

2 tablespoons soy sauce

2 tablespoons freshly squeezed lime juice

1 tablespoon allspice

1 tablespoon light brown sugar

2 teaspoons garlic powder

2 teaspoons dried thyme

2 teaspoons dried oregano

2 teaspoons onion powder

1 teaspoon freshly ground black pepper

1 teaspoon smoked paprika

¼ teaspoon ground cinnamon

¼ teaspoon freshly grated nutmeg

**Yield: 3 to 4 servings**

1 (4- to 5-pound) chicken, cut into quarters

1 tablespoon kosher salt

Steamed white or brown rice, for serving

1 cup Jerk Paste

1. Rinse the chicken thoroughly under cold running water and pat dry with paper towels.

2. Rub the chicken pieces with the jerk paste and place in a gallon-size resealable plastic bag or container. Allow to marinate under refrigeration for 2 to 24 hours.

3. Preheat oven to 425°F.

4. Arrange the chicken pieces on a baking sheet, leaving a little space between each piece. Bake for 10 minutes.

5. After 10 minutes, lower the heat to 350°F and continue to cook the chicken for about 30 minutes or until a thermometer placed in the thickest part of each piece registers 165°F. Be aware that the breast and wing quarters will probably be done a few minutes before the thigh and leg quarters.

6. Remove the pieces as they are done and allow the chicken to rest for about 5 minutes before serving.

7. Serve over steamed white or brown rice with some of the Tropical Fruit Salsa and a dollop of Scallion Aioli (recipes follow).

## Jerk Paste

Although at the restaurant we use this jerk paste primarily on chicken, it is wonderful on pork, beef, fish, and even shrimp and grilled vegetables.

Place all the ingredients in a food processor and pulse until the mixture becomes a chunky paste.

**NOTE:** Use gloves when handling hot peppers and wash your hands thoroughly afterward.

*(Continued)*

## Scallion Aioli

**Yield: about ¾ cup aioli**

1 cup chopped scallions

2 garlic cloves, peeled

2 tablespoons red wine vinegar

½ cup mayonnaise

¼ teaspoon kosher salt

⅛ teaspoon freshly ground black pepper

1. Place the scallions, garlic, and vinegar in a blender or food processor and pulse until everything is liquefied. Between pulses, you'll need to push the scallions back down into the blades with a rubber spatula or wooden spoon.

2. In a small bowl, blend the scallion purée and mayonnaise with a whisk and season with the salt and pepper.

## Tropical Fruit Salsa

**Yield: about 2½ cups salsa**

1 cup finely diced mango

1 cup finely diced pineapple

¼ cup finely diced red onion

¼ cup seeded and finely diced red bell pepper

¼ cup chopped fresh cilantro

2 tablespoons freshly squeezed lime juice

1 tablespoon extra-virgin olive oil

Combine all the ingredients in a small bowl.

# The Fried Chicken

There is no doubt that fried chicken is the star of the show at Hattie's. Day in, day out, year after year, whether we serve five or 500, half the people who walk in the door are going to order fried chicken. Some nights it seems like I could literally give away steak and lobster, and I would still serve 50 percent chicken. But that's OK; we have a different agenda at Hattie's.

People have been asking me for the recipe for years, and I usually give them the short version of what I'm going to try to explain now. It's not the recipe that matters. It couldn't be simpler. It's the process and the experience. It's developing a familiarity with the product, the process, and equipment until it becomes second nature. Until you can tell if the chicken is frying properly just by the sound it makes in the pan. As for experience. I'm not talking about how many chickens you have fried; the more the better. I'm talking about collective memory

*(Continued)*

experience. For most people who hold fried chicken near to their heart, it has more to do with a memory of a particular experience, than the chicken itself. For many, it may have been watching their mother or grandmother fry chicken in a cast-iron pan. When you think about that, you might start to remember the smell that would lazily drift though the house and the way that fragrance would make you salivate in anticipation of what was to come. For others, it may have been being brought to a restaurant like Hattie's. Either way, young or old, I can see it on the face of our customers when they walk in the door and again when they walk out. If we have done our job well, then we have either refreshed their past experience or planted the seed for the next generation of memories.

Experiment with the different types of frying setups I describe on page 248 and figure out which method you're most comfortable with. Once you settle on a method, plan on a few practice rounds before you start to see consistent results.

**Yield: 2 to 3 servings**

1 (2¾- to 3-pound) frying chicken, cut into 8 pieces

1 tablespoon kosher salt

2 teaspoons freshly ground black pepper

1 teaspoon garlic salt

Vegetable oil for frying (amount will vary, depending on the frying setup)

3 cups all-purpose flour

1. Rinse the chicken in a colander under cold running water and season with the salt, pepper, and garlic salt.

2. Heat the oil in your frying setup to 325°F.

3. Place the flour in a bowl or shallow dish and dredge the chicken so that it's thoroughly covered.

4. Carefully add the chicken to the oil one piece at time, making sure you don't crowd or overflow the pan. Cook for 10 to 12 minutes or until the chicken is fully cooked. Unless you're deep-frying, you will need to turn the chicken from time to time so it cooks evenly on both sides.

5. When the chicken is cooked, remove it from the oil and drain on paper towels. Make sure that the internal temperature reads at least 165°F. Repeat until all the chicken is cooked.

6. Allow the oil to cool completely before straining and storing.

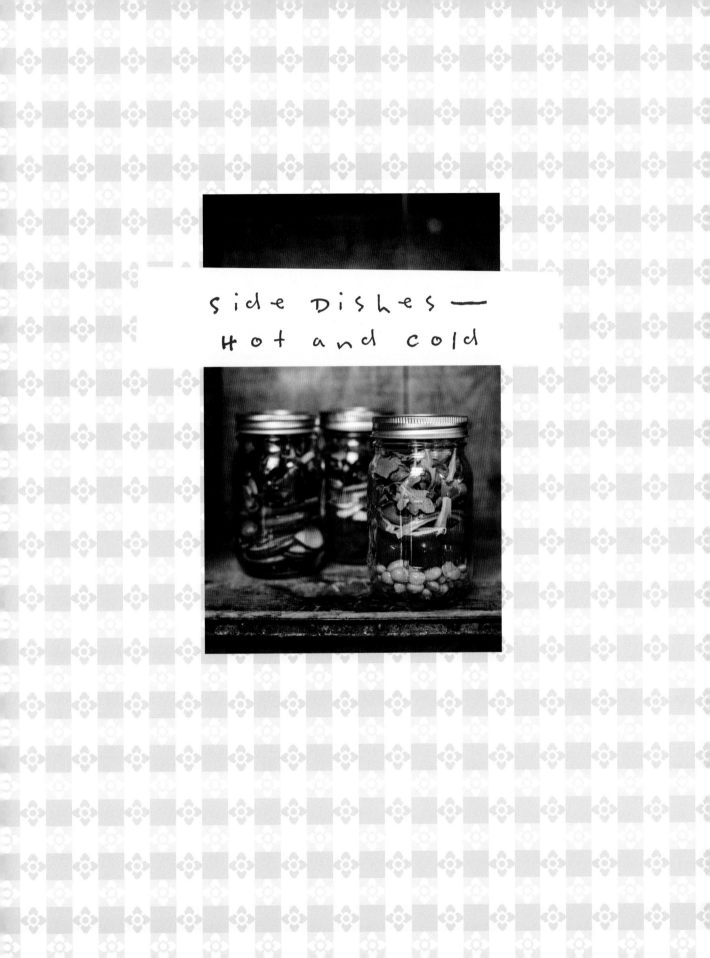

# side Dishes—
# Hot and cold

# Creamy Hominy

I was introduced to hominy at a very young age but it probably had less to do with my family's Southern roots than with the fact that we lived in San Diego. Hominy is as prevalent in Mexican and Native American cuisine as it is in Southern. Up here in the Northeast, I get a lot of, "Hominy? What's hominy?" Well, it's field corn boiled in a diluted alkaline solution. "Why do they do that?" is generally the next question. The key words here are *field corn*, which is far different from the varieties of sweet corn that most people immediately think of. Field corn is that decorative stuff that you hang on the door at Thanksgiving. Dry and hard as a rock, there is little use for it other than as animal feed, without processing it in one way or another. Anyway, I digress. Hominy is great stuff. It has a deep corn flavor and a fantastic dense, slightly chewy texture. When you combine hominy, the Cajun trinity (onion, celery, and bell pepper), and tomatoes, you have a versatile side dish that pairs well with roast chicken and pork dishes.

**Yield: 6 servings**

2 tablespoons olive oil

1 cup diced yellow onion

½ cup seeded and diced red bell pepper

½ cup seeded and diced green bell pepper

½ cup diced celery

1 tablespoon finely chopped garlic

2 teaspoons kosher salt

½ teaspoon freshly ground black pepper

¼ cup cider vinegar

2 (15-ounce) cans hominy, drained and rinsed

2 cups heavy cream

1 cup seeded and chopped tomato

1 tablespoon chopped fresh rosemary

1 tablespoon chopped fresh oregano

1 tablespoon chopped fresh parsley

¼ cup chopped scallions

1. Heat the olive oil in a 10-inch sauté pan or 4-quart saucepot over medium heat.

2. When the oil is shimmering, sauté the onion, bell peppers, and celery until they begin to get soft, about 5 minutes. Add the garlic, season with the salt and black pepper, and cook for an additional 2 minutes.

3. Add the vinegar and reduce by half.

4. Add the hominy and cream and simmer gently over medium heat until the cream has reduced by half, 5 to 10 minutes. Add the tomato, rosemary, and oregano and cook until the tomato is heated through, 1 to 2 minutes.

5. Garnish with the parsley and scallions.

## Smashed Potatoes

Mashed potatoes, whipped potatoes, potato puree, and yes, smashed potatoes. I hesitate to put yet another version of the potato classic into the world, but I would receive an endless amount of grief from our loyal customers if I neglected to include it. Our smashed potatoes are the most popular side dish we serve at Hattie's—during the summer months we average 100 to 150 pounds a night. I can't make it through the dining room without somebody asking, "What do you put in these mashed potatoes?" or "How much butter do you put in these potatoes? Wait, I don't want to know." OK, here is the big reveal . . . not much and lots. There is no magic here—just good potatoes, butter, salt, white pepper, and whole milk.

There are a few things you need to keep in mind when making any kind of mushed-up potatoes. First, potatoes love salt, and they love fat, and it helps to have a liquid medium to transfer their goodness into the potato.

Second, they don't respond well to mechanical mixing, so leave your mixer in the cabinet. Processing the potatoes by hand will practically eliminate the possibility of a gluey mash. Use an old-fashioned hand masher for a rustic smashed potato or a ricer or food mill if you are looking for a more refined mashed potato. As for peeling the potatoes, this is really a matter personal preference and desired end result. If you decide not to peel the potatoes, and at Hattie's we don't, you will need to give them a scrub with a vegetable brush to get the dirt off.

As far as the type of potato to use, we use a yellow-fleshed, heirloom potato called a Yellow Corolla that is grown for us by Sheldon Farms. Some potato applications require a specific potato selection, but mashed potatoes are pretty forgiving. Experiment with different varieties for subtle differences in texture and flavor.

Don't feel like your only options are butter and milk. You can use olive oil, bacon fat, sour cream, buttermilk, stock, yogurt, or cheese. The options are virtually endless.

**Yield: 8 to 10 servings**

3½ pounds scrubbed or peeled potatoes, cut into 2-inch pieces

3 tablespoons kosher salt, divided

2 cups whole milk

⅓ cup (6 tablespoons) unsalted butter

1 teaspoon freshly ground white or black pepper

1. Place the cut potatoes in a 6-quart stockpot and add enough cold water so that the potatoes are covered by at least 2 inches. Add 2 tablespoons of the salt and bring to a rolling boil over high heat. Once the water is boiling, lower the heat to maintain a vigorous simmer and cook until the potatoes are fork-tender, about 20 minutes.

2. While the potatoes are cooking, warm the milk and butter in a small saucepot over medium-low heat and keep warm.

3. When the potatoes are fork-tender, drain them into a colander. Allow the cooked potatoes to steam in the colander for 3 to 4 minutes. This step allows the potatoes to dry out a bit so they can absorb more milk and butter.

4. Return the potatoes to the pot you cooked them in if you're mashing by hand, or, process the hot potatoes through your ricer or food mill into the pot in small batches.

*(Continued)*

5. Pour the milk mixture over the potatoes in three or four batches, making sure to fully incorporate the liquid with a hand masher or rubber spatula between each batch. Scrape the bottom and corners of the pot once or twice to make sure there are no big lumps. Add as much of the liquid as possible without the potatoes becoming soupy. The total amount of liquid you add will vary slightly, depending on the variety of potatoes and exactly how long they were cooked.

6. Once you are happy with the texture, season with the remaining tablespoon of salt and the pepper.

# Creole Baked Beans

This is the perfect marriage of North and South. We have taken a few liberties with classic Boston baked beans by applying a little Creole sensibility and ended up with a dish that is both familiar and new. Like chili and most soups, this dish is best served the day after it's made, so that all the flavors have a chance to mingle. The pork that you use can vary, depending on what you like. Andouille sausage or tasso are both great choices, or for a milder but still smoky flavor, you can try smoked kielbasa. As I'm sure you have guessed by now, I'm a big fan of smoky pork products, so I have replaced the traditional fat back with a ham hock for some added smoky flavor. Anytime you cook dried beans, you should sort through them to ensure there are no rocks lurking about.

*(Continued)*

**Yield: 8 servings**

¼ cup olive oil

½ pound diced andouille sausage, tasso, or kielbasa

1 cup chopped onion

½ cup seeded and chopped green bell pepper

½ cup seeded and chopped red bell pepper

½ cup chopped celery

¼ cup finely chopped garlic

2 bay leaves

2 teaspoons dry mustard

1 teaspoon red chili flakes

1 teaspoon onion powder

1 teaspoon paprika

1 teaspoon chili powder

½ teaspoon cayenne pepper

1 tablespoon kosher salt

2 tablespoons tomato paste

2 cups chopped tomato, or 1 (14½-ounce) can diced tomatoes with juice

¼ cup light brown sugar

¼ cup cider vinegar

1 pound small dried red beans, soaked overnight in water and drained

1. Choose an 8-quart Dutch oven or heavy stockpot with a lid and position a rack in the lower portion of your oven so that the pot will fit comfortably in the oven with the lid on. Preheat oven to 300°F.

2. Heat the olive oil in the Dutch oven on the stove over medium heat.

3. When the oil is shimmering, add the andouille sausage and cook until golden brown, about 5 minutes. Add the onion, bell peppers, celery, and garlic and cook for an additional 5 minutes.

4. Add the bay leaves, spices, salt, tomato paste, tomato, brown sugar, and cider vinegar and cook for 2 to 3 minutes or until the sugar has dissolved.

5. Add the beans, stock, and ham hock and stir to combine. The stock should cover the beans by about 1 inch.

6. Bring the bean mixture up to a simmer, place the lid on the pot, and place the pot in your oven.

7. Cook the beans for 1½ to 2 hours, or until they are very tender, checking them about every 30 minutes or so to make sure they stay covered with stock. Stir the beans gently and add more stock, if necessary.

8. Remove the pot from the oven. Remove the ham hock and separate the meat with a pair of forks. Discard the bone and skin and return the meat to the beans. If you're going to serve the beans right away, add the herbs and serve.

4 cups chicken or vegetable stock, store-bought or homemade (pages 253 and 256), plus more as needed

1 ham hock

2 tablespoons chopped fresh rosemary

2 tablespoons chopped fresh oregano

½ cup chopped fresh parsley

9. If you're going to serve the beans at a later time, allow them to cool for 1 hour, then put the pot in refrigerator, uncovered, until fully cool. Once the beans are cool, cover with the lid or plastic wrap.

10. When you are ready to serve, reheat the beans over medium-low heat with more stock, if necessary, and add the rosemary and oregano. Serve topped with chopped parsley.

# Biscuits

Some Southerners, perhaps some in my own family, think that it's impossible for a Yankee to make good biscuits. They're wrong! The expense and scarcity of proper soft Southern red wheat flour, such as White Lily, does make the job a little tougher, but that doesn't mean our biscuits are tough. You can use cake flour, which like White Lily flour has a low protein and gluten content, or you can use all-purpose flour if you're careful. The single best piece of advice I can give is to watch how much you handle the dough. The more you work the dough, the more you will develop the gluten in the flour, and that will result in tough, chewy biscuits. To understand the subtleties of texture takes practice. Only by making biscuits by the hundreds every day for years have we achieved the consistently delicious results our customers expect. The perfect one-off biscuit is rare, like pink unicorn rare. Fortunately, biscuits are cheap, quick, and easy to make, so treat your family to some practice rounds, and you will have the technique down in no time.

**Yield: 20 medium biscuits**

1 pound flour (about 3 cups), plus more for dusting

1 tablespoon baking powder

1 tablespoon sugar

1 teaspoon salt

4 ounces chilled shortening, cut into ½-inch pieces

¾ cup buttermilk

¼ cup heavy cream

1. Preheat oven to 425°F and lightly grease a baking sheet with about a teaspoon of shortening or a light coating of cooking spray.

2. Sift the dry ingredients into a large bowl.

3. Cut in the shortening with a pastry cutter or your hands until there are no lumps larger than a pea.

4. In a separate bowl, mix the buttermilk and cream together.

5. Make a well in the center of the flour mixture with a spoon and add the buttermilk mixture while pulling flour down toward the center of the bowl until the liquid is just incorporated. The dough may seem a little wet. That's normal. Don't panic.

6. Scrape out the dough onto a well-floured surface and dust the top of the dough with a little more flour.

7. At this point, you should work the dough just enough that it is not sticky. Fold the mass toward you with your fingertips and allow it to pick up some of the flour from beneath it. You are not trying, nor should you try, to knead the dough as you would bread dough. You're just trying to get the proper texture and moisture level.

8. Once the dough is dry to the touch, use your hands or a rolling pin to flatten it down until it's about ¾ inch thick.

9. Using a cutter or a drinking glass, cut out the biscuits and arrange them on the prepared baking sheet so that their sides are just touching.

10. Bake for 15 to 20 minutes or until the biscuits are a light golden brown on the top.

# Corn and Tasso Spoon Bread

Tasso, or tasso ham as it is sometimes called, is not really ham at all but an aggressively seasoned and heavily smoked pork shoulder. It's very common in Cajun and Creole cuisine and almost interchangeable with andouille sausage for such dishes as gumbo and jambalaya. Unfortunately, outside of Louisiana it is not something you are likely to find at the corner grocery store. I'm beginning to see it more and more in specialty shops, and it's widely available online. At the restaurant, we get our tasso, andouille sausage, and bacon from North Country Smoke House in Claremont, New Hampshire. It's a family-run boutique smokehouse that really does a fine job across the board. While tasso does add a nice smoky heat to this dish, you can substitute any good-quality smoked ham with excellent results.

*(Continued)*

**Yield: 4 to 6 servings**

2 tablespoons unsalted butter at room temperature, divided, plus 1 teaspoon for buttering the baking dish

½ pound finely diced tasso

2½ cups milk

½ cup heavy cream

2 teaspoons sugar

½ teaspoon salt

1 cup cornmeal

4 large eggs, at room temperature, separated

2 cups corn kernels, fresh or frozen (thawed)

½ cup chopped scallions

1. Preheat oven to 350°F. Coat the bottom and sides of a 2-quart baking dish with 1 teaspoon of the butter.

2. Melt 1 tablespoon of butter in a sauté pan over medium heat and cook the tasso for about 5 minutes, or until golden brown. Transfer the tasso and any fat into a small bowl and set aside.

3. Combine the milk, cream, sugar, and salt in a 4-quart saucepot and bring to a simmer over medium heat.

4. Just as the liquid begins to simmer, reduce the heat to low and slowly add the cornmeal while whisking constantly. Cook for about 5 minutes, continuously whisking, until the cornmeal stops thickening and has a smooth texture. Remove from the heat. The mixture will look like thick mush.

5. Using a rubber spatula, fold in the remaining tablespoon of butter until fully absorbed by the cornmeal. Add the egg yolks, one at a time, while whisking vigorously. Be sure that each yolk is fully incorporated before adding the next yolk. Fold in the corn, tasso, and any reserved fat.

6. In a clean, medium bowl, beat the egg whites with a clean whisk or electric mixer until they form stiff peaks.

7. Using the rubber spatula, gently fold the egg whites into the cornmeal batter in three batches, making sure that each batch is fully incorporated before adding the next batch.

8. Transfer the mixture to the prepared baking dish and bake for 1 hour, or until the spoon bread is puffy and golden. Garnish with the chopped scallions.

## Basic Grits

Grits suffer a great paradox and are one of the most misunderstood Southern delicacies. They are basic sustenance to a Southerner, yet comic fodder for anyone outside the South. It goes much deeper than that, though. Most people without Southern roots don't even know what grits are, let alone whether they like them or not. It's not entirely their fault. If you live outside the South, you probably have only been exposed to instant or quick grits. Good news! You haven't really had grits, so it's time to come into the fold.

For clarity's sake, let's establish a few things. Real grits are stone-ground dried corn, period, end of story. Quick grits, whose germ and hull have been removed, or instant grits, which are cooked, dehydrated, and reground, have about as much in common with stone-ground grits as a loaf of naturally leavened French bread does with Wonder bread. They're just not the same thing.

*(Continued)*

Real grits are ground whole—hull, germ and all—and have delicious sweet corn flavor and a wonderfully creamy yet slightly grainy texture when cooked. They can be either white or yellow, based on the color of the corn they are made from. Yellow grits tend to have a more pronounced corn flavor and smoother texture than white grits. While you're still not likely to find stone-ground grits in your typical grocery store, they are generally available at health food stores and specialty groceries around the country. You can also order them easily online. Despite being dried, fresh stone-ground grits are quite perishable and should be stored in the refrigerator or freezer.

One of the best things about grits is their versatility. They can be cooked with water, milk, cream, or stock, depending on how you plan to use them. They can be made and served creamy or refrigerated and cut into shapes and fried, which gives them a nice crispy exterior. I've even cooked them in coconut milk and sugar and used them as a component to a dessert. They are great plain with just salt and butter, with cheese, or with bacon or country ham folded in. This recipe is creamy grits in their most basic form and provides an excellent base for experimentation for the grit novice.

**Yield: about 3 cups**

4 cups milk

2 bay leaves

1 cup uncooked stone-ground grits

2 tablespoons unsalted butter

2 teaspoons kosher salt

½ teaspoon freshly ground black pepper

1. Heat the milk and bay leaves to a boil in a 4-quart saucepot over medium-high heat. Try to catch it before it boils over.

2. Add the grits and lower the heat to medium. Whisk constantly until the mixture returns to a gentle simmer.

3. Reduce the heat to low so bubbles break the surface consistently but not vigorously. It should look like bubbling lava. Continue to cook, whisking frequently, for at least 30 to 45 minutes. The grits will continue to thicken the longer they cook, and you might need to add more milk or water, as necessary, to adjust the consistency for your particular taste or use. The longer you cook the grits and the more frequently you stir, the better they will be. Once your arm has given out, add the butter and adjust the seasoning with salt and pepper. Remove the bay leaves and serve.

# Cajun Coleslaw

This is a versatile, spicy slaw that can stand on its own or be part of any dish that calls for a creamy-style coleslaw with a little kick. This slaw was developed for the softshell crabs, but it earned most of its popularity as a component of the Fried Chicken Sandwich sold at Hattie's Track Shack and Hattie's Chicken Shack.

**Yield: 10 to 12 servings**

1 head (about 2 pounds) green cabbage, finely shredded

½ cup peeled and shredded carrot

2 teaspoons kosher salt

½ teaspoon freshly ground black pepper

½ cup sugar

½ cup cider vinegar, divided

½ cup pineapple juice

½ cup mayonnaise

2 tablespoons Hattie's Hot Rub (page 141) or commercial Cajun seasoning

2 tablespoons vegetable oil

¼ cup chopped fresh parsley

¼ cup chopped scallions

1. Combine the shredded cabbage and carrots with the salt, pepper, sugar, and ¼ cup of cider vinegar in a large bowl and mix thoroughly. Allow the slaw to sit at room temperature, turning it every now and again, for 1 to 2 hours so the cabbage will release some of its water.

2. Transfer the cabbage to a colander to drain. Squeeze the cabbage with both hands to remove any excess liquid and return it to the bowl.

3. Add the remaining ¼ cup of cider vinegar, and the pineapple juice, mayonnaise, Hattie's Hot Rub, vegetable oil, parsley, and scallions to the squeezed slaw and mix until well combined. Adjust the seasoning with salt and pepper, if necessary.

# Corn Bread

Along with the hundreds of biscuits we make every day at Hattie's, we are also constantly making corn bread. Everyone who sits down for supper gets a basket of corn bread and biscuits, so we go through a lot of corn bread. Corn bread, though common everywhere, is most popular in the South and the Southwest. So, you can imagine how, as a boy growing up largely in San Diego and of Southern heritage on both sides, I've been eating corn bread as long as I've been eating anything. At Hattie's our style of corn bread, like many things we do, lies somewhere between North and South. It does have a bit of sugar and some wheat flour, so I realize I might lose some purists right out of the gate. We will have to save the details of why for another book, but the reasons are similar to those of the plight of the over-refined grit. In both cases, modern milling practices remove too much of corn's properties and flavor from cornmeal in the name of profit, efficiency, and convenience.

**Yield: 8 to 10 servings**

3 cups cornmeal

1 cup all-purpose flour

2 tablespoons sugar

1 tablespoon baking powder

2 teaspoons kosher salt

2½ cups buttermilk

2 large eggs, beaten

⅓ cup (6 tablespoons) unsalted butter, melted, divided

1. Preheat oven to 350°F and place a 10-inch cast-iron pan or cake pan on the center rack to heat while you make the batter.

2. Combine the cornmeal, flour, sugar, baking powder, and salt in a large bowl.

3. In a separate bowl, combine the buttermilk, eggs, and 3 tablespoons of the melted butter.

4. Whisk the buttermilk mixture into the dry ingredients until just combined.

5. Remove the hot pan from the oven and pour in the remaining 3 tablespoons melted butter. Carefully swirl the butter around the pan to coat the bottom and sides.

6. Using a rubber spatula, scrape the batter evenly into the hot buttered pan and return the pan to the oven.

7. Bake for 20 to 25 minutes, or until a toothpick or paring knife inserted into the center of the corn bread comes out clean.

# Cranberry Coleslaw

Except for fried chicken, Cranberry Coleslaw is the most frequently requested recipe at Hattie's. It's on the menu only during the summer at the original restaurant, but we offer it year-round at the Chicken Shack and also have it on the menu at the Track Shack. Because the dressing is vinegar based, this coleslaw is a crunchy, refreshing alternative to the more common mayonnaise-based slaws. One of the tricks to good coleslaw, especially a vinegar-based slaw, is to brine the cabbage first for an hour or two and then squeeze out some of the water. This draws out some of the bitter, excess water from the cabbage, so it can be discarded and not affect the flavor balance or consistency of the finished slaw.

1. Combine the shredded cabbage and carrot with the sugar, salt, pepper, and ½ cup of the cider vinegar in a large bowl and mix thoroughly. Allow the slaw to sit at room temperature, turning it every now and again, for 1 to 2 hours so the cabbage will release some of its water.

2. Transfer the cabbage to a colander to drain. Squeeze the cabbage with both hands to remove any excess liquid and return it to the bowl.

3. Add the remaining ¼ cup of vinegar, cranberries, oil, parsley, and scallions to the squeezed slaw and mix until well combined. Adjust the seasoning with salt and pepper, if necessary.

**Yield: 10 to 12 servings**

1 head (about 2 pounds) green cabbage, finely shredded

½ cup peeled and shredded carrot

¾ cup sugar

2 teaspoons kosher salt

½ teaspoons freshly ground black pepper

¾ cup cider vinegar, divided

1½ cups dried cranberries

2 tablespoons vegetable oil

¼ cup chopped fresh parsley

¼ cup chopped scallions

## Dirty Rice

This is a great dish for people who are lukewarm about chicken livers. The small amount of liver in this dish is just enough to provide a rich undercurrent of flavor without dominating. There are a lot of strong flavors in this dish, so if you don't tell people there is liver in it, I bet they won't even notice. It's a substantial side dish or can stand on its own for a light supper. At the restaurant, I have served it as an appetizer, a side dish, and as an accompaniment to a variety of chicken and pork dishes.

This recipe is a great way to use the leftover rice you have from the Chinese food you ordered the other night. After all, when you get right down to it, dirty rice is really just Southern fried rice. But freshly cooked rice works fine, too, and if you want, you can put a twist on it by using brown or wild rice.

**Yield: 4 to 6 servings**

2 tablespoons olive oil

4 ounces sliced bacon, cut into ½-inch pieces

4 ounces chicken livers, cut into ¼- to ½-inch pieces

½ cup diced onion

¼ cup seeded and diced green bell pepper

¼ cup seeded and diced red bell pepper

¼ cup diced celery

1 teaspoon chopped garlic

1 cup corn kernels, fresh or frozen (thawed)

4 cups cooked rice, leftover or freshly cooked

1 teaspoon kosher salt

½ teaspoon freshly ground black pepper

2 tablespoons chopped fresh parsley

2 tablespoons chopped scallions

1. Heat the oil in a 10- to 12-inch nonstick skillet over medium-low heat.

2. Render and brown the bacon, about 5 minutes.

3. Increase the heat to medium, add the chicken livers, and cook for 1 to 2 minutes.

4. Add the onion, bell peppers, celery, and garlic and sauté for 3 to 4 minutes. Add the corn and continue to sauté for an additional 5 minutes.

5. Add the rice. If you're using cold leftover rice, cook for an additional 5 minutes, or until the rice is hot. If you use hot rice, you just need to break it up gently and incorporate into the liver mixture.

6. Season with salt and black pepper and garnish with the parsley and scallions.

# Collard Greens

The recipe for collard greens at Hattie's has been the same as long as anyone can remember. Our longtime dishwasher and historian in residence, Ernest Waters, passed it on to me. Ernie began working with Hattie when he was in high school and remained at the restaurant for more than 35 years. I had the honor of working with Ernie for the first 10 years we owned the restaurant, and he has provided invaluable insight into the restaurant's early years and helped anchor the continuity between past and present.

The collard recipe is somewhat unusual in that it's a bit sweet and doesn't contain pork. This keeps our vegetarian patrons happy and also keeps tradition alive.

The cooking time of collard greens can vary considerably, depending on when they are harvested. They can take as little as 45 minutes to upwards of 3 hours, so taste them along the way and pronounce them done when you're happy with the texture.

**Yield: 6 servings**

2 bunches collard greens, stemmed and torn into 2-inch pieces (about 12 cups loosely packed)

¼ cup olive oil

2 cups medium-diced onion

1 tablespoon kosher salt

½ teaspoon freshly ground black pepper

¼ cup Worcestershire sauce

¼ cup cider vinegar

½ cup sugar

1 teaspoon Louisiana-style hot sauce

2 cups water

1. Wash the greens in a colander or salad spinner. It is not necessary to get all the water off the greens.

2. Heat the oil in a large stockpot over medium heat. When the oil is shimmering, sauté onions for 5 minutes, or until they are translucent.

3. Add the collard greens to the pot in two or three batches, allowing the first batch to wilt slightly before adding the next batch, season with salt and pepper, and sauté for 5 minutes or until the greens start to break down and lose some of their volume.

4. Add the Worcestershire, cider vinegar, sugar, hot sauce, and water and bring the mixture to a simmer. Stir frequently so that the greens settle down into the pot liquor. Once the pot liquor is simmering, reduce the heat to maintain a low simmer and place a lid on the pot. Stir every 15 to 20 minutes, until the desired texture is achieved.

# Salad Dressing
# (and Mason Jar Salad)

For many years, like 60 or so, there was only one salad dressing made at Hattie's. It has been a staple on the menu as long as anyone can remember and predated my arrival by my entire life plus a decade or two. The salad dressing was always something that Ernie made. A few months into our tenure, when we ran out on a night that he wasn't working, I realized I'd better watch how he made it and get it down on paper. What I learned was that it didn't come close to having the normal ratios of oil and vinegar found in most vinaigrettes. What I know is that it's sweet and delicious and possesses a comforting homeyness. For me it was like something you had at your grandmother's as a child, completely forgot, and then tasted again as an adult, bringing back all the associated memories. We still use this vinaigrette on our Chopped Mason Jar Salad, where we add all the ingredients—including the salad dressing—to a mason jar, shake it up tableside, and allow the customer to release the contents into a bowl. As for the salad itself, what we serve varies with the seasons. Lettuces mixed with cucumbers, radishes, baby turnips, carrots, tomatoes, red onion, sugar snap peas—anything that is in season will work.

Presentation is the key. Layer the hardier vegetables toward the bottom and the lettuces on the top, paying attention to color and texture.

**Yield: about 2½ cups dressing**

1 cup cider vinegar

1 cup sugar

¼ cup vegetable oil

1 tablespoon dried oregano

½ teaspoon kosher salt

¼ teaspoon freshly ground black pepper

1.  Combine the cider vinegar and sugar in a medium bowl and whisk until the sugar has dissolved.

2.  Add the oil, oregano, salt, and pepper and whisk to combine. The dressing will keep almost indefinitely in an airtight container stored in the refrigerator.

# Candied Sweet Potatoes

Candied sweet potatoes have been a staple on the winter menu at Hattie's for some time. Typically a Southern candied sweet potato recipe would have some combination of cane syrup, molasses, or sorghum syrup as a component of the glaze, but since we are in prime maple syrup country up here in the Northeast, I have made what I believe is an appropriate regional substitution. If you want a more traditional Southern style, you can substitute 1½ cups of cane syrup or light corn syrup and ½ cup of molasses or sorghum syrup for the maple syrup. If you have only used ground nutmeg in the past, do yourself a favor and try grating your own from whole nutmeg—the flavor is far superior.

**Yield: 8 to 10 servings**

2 teaspoons unsalted butter at room temperature

1 cup firmly packed light brown sugar

1½ cups pure maple syrup

½ cup molasses

1 cup freshly squeezed orange juice

⅛ teaspoon freshly grated nutmeg

⅛ teaspoon ground allspice

½ teaspoon ground cinnamon, or 2 cinnamon sticks

3 pounds sweet potatoes, peeled and cut into 1-inch dice

2 tablespoons chopped fresh parsley

1. Preheat oven to 400°F.

2. Coat the bottom and sides of a 3-quart baking dish with the butter.

3. Combine the brown sugar, maple syrup, molasses, orange juice, nutmeg, allspice, and cinnamon in a large bowl and stir with a whisk.

4. Add the sweet potatoes, toss to coat evenly, and pour into the prepared baking dish.

5. Roast for about 1 hour, or until the potatoes are fork-tender and have a glazed sheen to them. Stir and turn over the sweet potatoes occasionally to ensure even cooking. If it looks as though the potatoes are getting dry or too dark, add a little more orange juice and give them a stir.

6. Garnish with the chopped parsley.

# Cucumber Salad

Like cranberry coleslaw, cucumber salad is on the menu only during the summer at the original restaurant, but we offer it year-round at the Chicken Shack and at the Track Shack during racing season. The finished salad is very refreshing, a pleasant balance of sweet and sour with red onion providing a nice bite. Once the cucumbers have had time to react to vinegar and sugar, they take on a texture similar to that of bread-and-butter pickles. It takes a minimum of 2 hours for the vinegar, sugar, and salt to have any real effect on the cucumbers. Letting the salad marinate for 4 to 5 hours, or even overnight, is better. When our growing season kicks in, we get all our cucumbers from my good friend Albert Sheldon, who owns Sheldon Farm in Salem, New York. Getting fresh cucumbers from your local farmers' market will make a big difference in flavor.

1. Combine all the ingredients in a large bowl and marinate, refrigerated, for at least 2 hours, tossing every now and again.

2. If the salad tastes a little watery after it has marinated, it's because of all the water that has been pulled out of the cucumbers. Pour some of the liquid out, refresh with a little more red wine vinegar and sugar, then recheck the seasoning and adjust, if necessary.

**Yield: 4 to 6 servings**

5 cucumbers, peeled or not, sliced ⅛-inch thick

1 cup thinly sliced red onion

1 cup red wine vinegar

½ cup sugar

1 tablespoon kosher salt

1 teaspoon freshly ground black pepper

2 teaspoons vegetable oil

¼ cup chopped fresh parsley

¼ cup chopped scallions

# Savory Corn Bread Pudding

Bread puddings, whether sweet or savory, are a great way to use up leftover bread. This Southern version uses corn bread and pork sausage, but you could omit the sausage if you want to make it vegetarian. We make corn bread every day at Hattie's, so we always have some around, but this is good enough that it's worth making corn bread just for the pudding. All bread puddings are better made with stale bread, so it's nice to use corn bread that's a couple of days old and a little dried out. If you use fresh corn bread, it may crumble a bit more, making the texture more homogeneous, but it will still be delicious.

**Yield: 6 servings**

1 teaspoon unsalted butter at room temperature

5 cups cubed corn bread (½-inch cubes), store-bought or homemade (page 177)

1 cup grated extra-sharp cheddar cheese

2 tablespoons olive oil

1 pound bulk pork sausage

1 cup chopped onion

1 cup corn kernels, fresh or frozen (thawed)

1 cup chopped scallions

6 large eggs

2 cups heavy cream

1 cup milk

2 teaspoons kosher salt

1 teaspoon freshly ground black pepper

1 tablespoon chopped fresh parsley

1 tablespoon chopped fresh thyme

1 tablespoon chopped fresh rosemary

1 tablespoon chopped fresh sage

1. Preheat oven to 350°F. Prepare an 8-inch square baking dish by coating the bottom and sides with the butter. Place the corn bread cubes and cheese in a large bowl.

2. Heat the olive oil in a heavy, 10-inch sauté pan over medium heat. When the oil is shimmering, brown the sausage, breaking up the larger chunks until the sausage is fully cooked, about 10 minutes. Remove the pan from the heat, transfer the sausage with a slotted spoon to the bowl containing the corn bread, and give the mixture a quick stir to combine. Pour out most of the sausage drippings, leaving only 2 to 3 tablespoons in the pan.

3. Return the pan to the stove and sauté the onion in the sausage drippings over medium heat for 5 to 10 minutes or until the onion is soft and beginning to brown. Add the corn and scallions and cook for an additional 2 minutes, then add to the corn bread mixture.

4. Combine the eggs, cream, milk, salt, and pepper in a medium mixing bowl and whisk until well incorporated.

5. Pour the custard over the corn bread mixture, add the herbs, and gently blend all the ingredients together. Allow the mixture to sit for 5 to 10 minutes so the corn bread has a chance to absorb the custard.

6. Transfer the pudding to the baking dish and bake for about 40 minutes or until the custard is set and the top is golden brown.

## Hoppin' John Salad

For as long as I can remember, my family has had some sort of pork, greens, and black-eyed peas for New Year's Day dinner. This is a Southern tradition to ensure health, wealth, and happiness for the coming year. This salad is inspired by that tradition and provides a delicious summery twist on the New Year's Day classic. Consider it a booster shot for the second half of the year.

**Yield: 8 to 10 servings**

4 cups cooked black-eyed peas (from 2 cups dried) or canned

3 tablespoons vegetable or olive oil

2 cups diced ham (¼-inch dice)

2 cups corn kernels, fresh or frozen (thawed)

1 cup finely chopped onion

½ cup seeded and finely chopped red bell pepper

½ cup seeded and finely chopped green bell pepper

1 tablespoon finely chopped garlic

2 teaspoons kosher salt

½ teaspoon freshly ground black pepper

6 cups cooked rice

1 cup extra-virgin olive oil

Juice and zest of 2 lemons

1 tablespoon Old Bay Seasoning

1 cup chopped scallions

½ cup chopped fresh parsley

¼ cup chopped fresh cilantro

1. Rinse and drain the cooked or canned black-eyed peas in a colander under running water.

2. Heat the oil in an 8-inch sauté pan over medium heat. Add the ham and sauté for about 3 minutes.

3. Add the corn, onion, bell peppers, and garlic, season with salt and black pepper, and sauté for 5 minutes or until the vegetables are tender but still have a little bite. Transfer the vegetables to a large bowl.

4. Add the drained black-eyed peas and the rice to the bowl with the vegetables and mix with a spoon.

5. Sprinkle the olive oil, lemon juice and zest, and Old Bay over the rice mixture while stirring so that they are evenly distributed.

6. This salad can be made and served immediately or up to 2 days in advance. If you make it in advance, remove the salad from the refrigerator 1 hour before serving and mix it a few times as it is coming to room temperature to redistribute the liquids that will have settled to the bottom. Add the scallions, parsley, and cilantro just before serving.

# Breakfast and Brunch

## The World's Best Egg Sandwich

You may think you've already had the world's best egg sandwich. Maybe you have; maybe this recipe won't move the needle for you. But if you think it has a chance, it's worth a little time and effort. For its charms to work, you're going to have to like bacon, and not just any bacon, but caramelized bacon. It will also help if you like avocado. It enhances the texture and provides balance of flavor. You will, at the very least, need to accept that American cheese, while not even technically a cheese, has its place, and one of them is in this sandwich. You will also need to make the English Muffin Bread. I know, I dropped the baking bomb at the end, but this is where it all comes together. Do not be discouraged. It's super easy even for someone who doesn't bake, I promise. Will the sandwich be good if you don't make the bread? Yes, but not as good. I know what you're thinking, *I'll just swap out the bread for English muffins.* Nope, it's not the same, we tried. We started by making our own English muffins, which evolved into the English Muffin Bread. In the end, it's not about actually being the best, it's about striving to be the best.

**Yield: 4 sandwiches**

8 (½-inch-thick) slices English Muffin Bread (recipe follows)

12 slices American cheese

2 avocados, peeled, pitted, and smashed with a fork, then sprinkled with a squeeze of lemon juice and a pinch of salt

12 slices caramelized bacon (recipe follows), cut in half

8 large eggs

1. Preheat oven on BROIL. Arrange the bread slices on a baking sheet and toast both sides. Place 1½ slices of the cheese on each piece of bread and put the baking sheet back into the oven to melt the cheese.

2. On half the bread pieces, spread a nice layer of avocado on top of the cheese; then evenly distribute the bacon on the remaining 4 pieces of bread.

3. Fry or scramble your eggs and place on top of the bacon. Top with the other slices.

## Caramelized Bacon

You obviously are not going to need a whole pound of bacon for this sandwich, but I'm factoring that a couple of pieces might go missing. Cooking the bacon in the oven works far better than a pan, especially with the added sugar that would likely burn in the pan.

**Yield: 1 pound bacon**

¼ cup light brown sugar

2 tablespoon Hattie's Hot Rub (page 141) or commercial Cajun seasoning

1 pound thick-cut bacon

1. Preheat oven to 350°F. Line a baking sheet with parchment or aluminum foil.

2. Mix together the brown sugar and Hattie's Hot Rub in a small bowl.

3. Lay the bacon on the prepared baking sheet so that slices are not touching. Sprinkle both sides with the spice mixture. Bake until the bacon is a deep golden brown and crispy. Drain on a paper towel and keep warm.

# English Muffin Bread

This recipe makes two loaves, and I'm guessing that once you taste it, you'll be happy that you have the extra loaf. It's fabulous with butter and jam or anything else you like to spread on toast.

**Yield: 2 loaves bread**

¾ cup cornmeal, divided

5½ cups all-purpose flour, divided, plus more for dusting

1 ounce active dry yeast

1½ tablespoons sugar

1 tablespoon salt

½ teaspoon baking soda

2 cups milk

1 cup water

1. Prepare two standard 8 x 4½ x 2¾-inch loaf pans by coating them with pan spray and pouring ¼ cup of the cornmeal into one of the loaf pans. Gently shake the pan to coat the bottom and sides and lightly tap the excess into the second loaf pan. Repeat the process and discard the excess cornmeal.

2. In a large bowl or stand mixer, combine the remaining ½ cup of cornmeal, 2 cups of the flour, yeast, sugar, salt, and baking soda. Mix with a whisk or using your mixer's paddle attachment on low speed.

3. Warm the milk and water in a small sauté pan until it's just above body temperature, about 100°F.

4. Combine the warm liquid with the dry ingredients and mix thoroughly, scraping down the bottom and sides of the bowl. Add the remaining 3½ cups of flour, 1 cup at a time, and mix until well combined. At this stage it's going to look more like stiff batter than bread dough.

5. Turn out the dough onto a floured surface and, with floured hands or a spoon, divide the dough equally between the loaf pans and cover loosely with a towel or plastic wrap. Place the pans in a warm spot in your kitchen and allow to rise for about 45 minutes or until the dough has doubled in size. While the dough is rising, preheat oven to 375°F.

6. Bake for about 30 minutes or until golden brown. Remove from the loaf pans and cool on a wire cooling rack.

# Beignets

Beignets are a French market doughnut served in many of the coffee-houses in New Orleans. The most popular of these coffeehouses, Café Du Monde, is worth a trip to New Orleans all on its own. Beignets are sweet yeast dough, typically cut into squares, fried, and covered with a mountain of powdered sugar. At the original Hattie's, we serve them on the brunch menu as a starter and occasionally for dessert on the dinner menu. We will also put a savory twist on them by stuffing them with andouille sausage or pimento cheese and serving them as an appetizer. At the Chicken Shack, we serve them all day every day and always have a batch or two proofing in the walk-in cooler. This dough needs to proof overnight in the refrigerator, so you will need to make it the day before you are going to have your beignets. This recipe will make a few dozen beignets and it is hard to make a smaller batch, so invite some friends over. If you don't want to share your beignets, that's OK. The dough will last for a few days in the fridge, so you can cut off what you need and use the remaining dough later.

*(Continued)*

**Yield: about 4 dozen beignets**

1½ cups warm water

1 (¼-ounce) package active dry yeast

½ cup sugar, divided

1 teaspoon kosher salt

2 large eggs, beaten

1 cup evaporated milk

7 cups all-purpose flour, divided, plus about 1 cup for dusting

¼ cup vegetable shortening

Vegetable oil for frying

Lots of powdered sugar, about 1 cup per dozen, or even more

1. In a large bowl, combine the warm water, yeast, and 1 tablespoon of the sugar and whisk until the yeast has dissolved. Set the bowl aside and wait for about 5 minutes for some bubbles to appear on the surface of the water as an indication that the yeast is active and working.

2. While you're waiting for the yeast, combine the remaining sugar, salt, eggs, and evaporated milk in a small bowl and whisk together.

3. Add the egg mixture to the yeast mixture and mix thoroughly with a whisk. Add 3½ cups of the flour and mix with a wooden spoon until fully incorporated. Add the shortening in little globs the size of a marble and work into the dough with the spoon.

4. Work in the remaining 3½ cups of flour about ½ cup at a time. The dough will become very stiff. Cover the bowl with plastic and put in the refrigerator overnight to proof.

5. Sprinkle about ½ cup of flour on a clean, dry work surface. Turn the dough out of the bowl and sprinkle a little more flour on top of the dough.

6. Roll the dough with a rolling pin to a thickness of ⅛ inch and then cut into 2 x 3-inch rectangles. Add more flour as necessary to prevent sticking.

7. Preheat oven to 200°F and preheat your preferred frying setup to 350°F. You will need at least 2 to 3 inches of oil.

8. Fry the beignets a few at a time, cooking them for 2 to 3 minutes on each side or until golden brown. The beignets will start to puff up as soon as they hit the hot oil, so you will need to flip them over a few times to help them brown evenly.

9. Carefully remove the beignets from the oil, using a pair of tongs or a slotted spoon, and place on a baking sheet lined with paper towels. Keep them in the oven while you fry the rest of the beignets.

10. Sprinkle what you think is enough powdered sugar over your hot beignets and then double it.

## Two-Potato Ham Hash

When it comes to breakfast, my personal taste tends to gravitate toward a few categories, with hash near the top of the list. There is a lot of regional variation on the theme, and even when it's delicious it can fall flat outside that specific region. For instance, in Seattle we served smoked salmon hash. It sold like crazy. Here in the Northeast, nothing. Cue the cricket sound effects. I switched to smoked trout, figuring it would be more regionally appropriate. More crickets and the lonely hoot of an owl. The first version of this two-potato hash used traditional Southern salt-cured country ham, but customers perceived its beautiful salty essence as too salty. We switched to a more traditional cured and smoked ham, and bingo, we had a winner. I like a hash with substance, bigger pieces of crispy potato, vegetables with a little char around the edge, and earthy herb and spice undertones. We serve this hash for brunch alongside eggs, but it's versatile enough to be used as a side dish for dinner as well.

**Yield: 4 to 6 servings**

2 cups peeled, diced russet potatoes (½-inch dice)

2 cups peeled, diced sweet potatoes (½-inch dice)

2 tablespoons white or cider vinegar

3 tablespoons kosher salt, divided

¼ cup olive oil

1 cup chopped yellow onion

½ cup seeded and chopped red bell pepper

½ cup seeded and chopped poblano chili

3 cloves chopped garlic

3 cups diced smoked ham (½-inch dice)

1 teaspoon freshly ground black pepper

½ cup chopped scallions

¼ cup chopped fresh parsley

1 tablespoon chopped fresh rosemary

1 tablespoon chopped fresh thyme

8–12 large eggs

1. Place the potatoes and sweet potatoes in a 4-quart saucepan with the vinegar, 2 tablespoons of the salt, and enough cold water to cover the potatoes by 1 inch. Bring to a boil over high heat, lower the heat, and simmer for 5 minutes or until the potatoes are just starting to get tender. Drain in a colander, set aside, and allow to steam until needed.

2. Heat a large, cast-iron, or heavy-gauge skillet over medium-high heat. Pour in the oil, and when it just begins to smoke, add the potatoes and spread evenly around the pan. Cook the potatoes for about 5 minutes or until they start to brown. Turn the potatoes once or twice so they brown evenly without burning, but don't fuss with them too much.

3. Add the yellow onion, pepper, and chili to the potatoes and continue to cook for about 10 minutes, turning occasionally, until the potatoes are crispy and the vegetables have a bit of char around the edges.

4. Add the garlic and ham and continue to cook for 3 to 5 minutes or until the ham is hot. Stir in the remaining tablespoon of salt, the black pepper, and the scallions and herbs, then remove from the heat.

5. Serve with eggs cooked the way you like them (see note).

NOTE: As an alternative, you could bake the eggs in the hash for a one-pot meal. Preheat oven to 350°F. Make a few wells in the hash with the back of a spoon and crack the eggs into the wells. Place the pan in the oven for 5 to 7 minutes, or until the eggs have baked to your preferred level of doneness.

# Andouille, Caramelized Onion, and Cheddar Omelet

This is one of the most popular items on Hattie's brunch menu. The combination of the sweet caramelized onions and the spicy andouille sausage is rich and satisfying. Add some good-quality extra-sharp cheddar and, well . . . cheese makes just about everything better.

**Yield: 1 serving**

3 large eggs

2 tablespoons cream or milk

1 tablespoon olive oil

½ cup finely chopped onion

½ teaspoon kosher salt

¼ cup finely chopped andouille sausage

3 tablespoons grated extra-sharp cheddar cheese

1 tablespoon chopped fresh parsley

1 tablespoon chopped scallions

1. Beat the eggs and cream or milk together in a small bowl and set aside.

2. Heat a 6-inch nonstick sauté pan over medium heat. Pour in the olive oil, and when it's shimmering, add the onion and salt and sauté until the onion is medium brown in color, about 10 minutes. The goal is to caramelize the sugars in the onion to bring out its natural sweetness.

3. Add the andouille sausage and continue to cook until the sausage is golden brown and hot, about 5 minutes.

4. Pour the egg mixture into the pan. As the eggs begin to set, pull them away from the sides while tilting the pan left and right, allowing the remaining egg mixture to coat the bottom.

5. When most of the egg has set, sprinkle the cheese over the top of the omelet and fold it in half with a rubber spatula.

6. Reduce the heat to low and continue to cook until the cheese has melted. Slide the omelet onto a plate and garnish with the parsley and scallions.

## Biscuits and Sausage Gravy

Ahh, biscuits and sausage gravy, the granddaddy of all Southern breakfast dishes. The light at the end of the dark and lonely tunnel of a hangover. Responsible for pulling countless people back from the edge. For my money, there is no dish with more restorative power than a good plate of biscuits and gravy. So simple it almost doesn't need a recipe, yet worthy of one due to the likelihood that at some point it may be the only thing standing between you and the slow, agonizing pain of a day lost to overindulgence. There are only three ingredients in sausage gravy and two of them are fairly standard, so your focus should be on the sausage. Buy fresh, plain, bulk pork breakfast sausage. Maple links and Italian sausage have their place, but it's not here. Sauté your sausage carefully, nice and easy; brown it too hard and your finished gravy may taste and look darker than it should. Lower the heat even more when you add the flour. You're going for a blond roux here. Add the milk and bring to a simmer slowly, whisking frequently to keep the roux from burning on the bottom of the pan. Too close to let the gravy get away from you now. Ten minutes at a low simmer to cook out the floury taste of the roux and you're ready for the warm hug from your new best friend.

**Yield: 4 servings**

1 tablespoon unsalted butter

1 pound plain bulk pork breakfast sausage

⅓ cup all-purpose flour

3 to 4 cups milk

1 tablespoon kosher salt

½ teaspoon freshly ground black pepper

4 Biscuits (page 168)

1. Preheat a heavy-gauge, 2-quart saucepot or sauté pan over medium-low heat.

2. Toss in the butter, and when it's melted and bubbling, add the sausage. Break the sausage up a bit as it browns. You don't want giant chunks, but you don't want the sausage to have the texture of hamburger, either.

3. When the sausage is fully cooked but not dark brown, reduce the heat to low and add the flour.

4. Whisk the flour for 2 to 3 minutes so it absorbs the fat rendered from the sausage and forms a light pan roux.

5. Add the milk and season with the salt and pepper. Slowly bring the mixture to a simmer, whisking frequently, and simmer for 10 to 15 minutes or until you have cooked out the floury taste of the roux.

6. Split your biscuits in half and warm them in a toaster or oven. Place the bottom half of the biscuits on a plate; ladle a generous portion of gravy over the top, and sandwich with the other half of the biscuit.

7. Grab a fork.

# Buttermilk Pancakes and Waffles

The pancakes we make at Hattie's are some of the best you'll ever eat. As a busy parent of two I can understand the time-saving lure of a pre-made pancake mix, but this batter will only take a few seconds longer to put together and is far superior. The key to light and fluffy pancakes is to not overmix the batter. It is desirable to have some lumps, and if you beat the batter until it's smooth your pancakes will be anything but light and fluffy. You can add berries, bananas, nuts, chocolate chips, or whatever else suits your fancy, to jazz them up. These items should be added to the pancakes once they are on the griddle and the batter is bubbling, just before you flip them. If your kids are having a sleepover and you know you're going to be working the griddle for the masses in the morning, you can make the batter the night before and keep it in the refrigerator. Although any nonstick pan will work, a cast-iron or electric griddle is the best option.

**Yield: 8 to 10 (3- to 4-inch) pancakes**

3 cups all-purpose flour

1 tablespoon baking powder

1½ teaspoons baking soda

½ teaspoon salt

¼ cup sugar

3 large eggs, beaten

3 cups buttermilk

¼ cup melted unsalted butter

1 teaspoon vegetable oil, plus more as needed

1. In a large bowl, sift together all the dry ingredients and make a well in the center.

2. In a separate bowl, whisk the eggs and buttermilk together until well combined.

3. Pour the egg mixture into the center of the well and combine gently, using a whisk. Halfway through mixing the wet and dry ingredients together, add the melted butter. Do not overmix.

4. If you're using an electric griddle, preheat it to 350° to 375°F. If you're using a cast-iron griddle, start with medium heat and adjust as necessary. Drizzle a little oil on your griddle.

5. Pour about ¼ cup of batter onto the griddle for each pancake. After bubbles begin to break the surface and the bottom is golden brown, flip the pancakes and continue to cook for about 2 more minutes.

**NOTE:** The recipe for waffles is the same, but the process changes slightly. Instead of adding the whole eggs to the buttermilk, separate the eggs, adding the yolks to the buttermilk. In a separate bowl, whisk the egg whites to stiff peaks and fold them gently into the batter, using a rubber spatula. To cook, follow the instructions for your waffle maker.

## Pain Perdu

Pain perdu is the New Orleans version of French toast. Translated, it means "lost bread" and is a great way to use leftover French bread that otherwise might get lost to the garbage can. Besides saving you money and another trip to the store, having the bread a little dried out and stale actually produces a better product than fresh bread. It readily absorbs the custard without getting too soft and falling apart. We serve this at the restaurant for brunch, and I'll typically go to the bakery on Wednesday or Thursday to get the bread for the weekend.

I like to cook the pain perdu a little longer than you might cook typical French toast. This allows the sugar in the custard to caramelize and make a crisp exterior, which contrasts nicely to the soft, rich interior. You're going to need a large cast-iron or nonstick pan or an electric griddle. If you're cooking for a crowd, heat oven to 200°F to keep the first rounds warm while you cook the remaining slices.

**Yield: 4 servings**

1 cup milk

1 cup heavy cream

4 large eggs, beaten

½ cup sugar

½ teaspoon pure vanilla extract

Juice and zest of 1 orange

2 tablespoons vegetable oil, plus more as needed

8 (1-inch-thick) slices French bread

2 tablespoons powdered sugar

Pure maple syrup, for serving

1. In a large bowl combine the milk, cream, eggs, granulated sugar, vanilla, and orange juice and zest. Mix with a whisk until the ingredients are thoroughly combined. If you wish, this can be done the night before and stored in the refrigerator.

2. Dip two or three slices of bread into the custard. The amount of time you allow the bread to soak in the custard will depend on how dried-out the bread is. You want the bread to absorb enough custard to be soft and rich, but not so much that it's falling apart. By starting with just a few slices, you will be able to test the soaking time and make adjustments, if necessary.

3. Preheat your pan over medium-high heat or your electric griddle to 350° to 375°F. When the pan or griddle is hot, add the vegetable oil.

4. Cook the soaked bread slices a few at a time, without crowding the pan, until they are a deep golden brown on each side. Serve immediately or keep warm by placing the cooked slices in a 200°F oven.

5. Sprinkle a little powdered sugar over the top of the slices and serve with pure maple syrup.

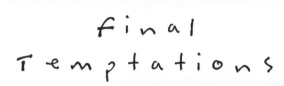

# final Temptations

## Sweet Potato Pie

When my wife, Beth, was working as a waitress at Hattie's in the mid-1990s, her classic line was, "Now, you can't leave without trying a piece of Miss Hattie's sweet potato pie." The line worked and she sold a ton of sweet potato pie. Not much has changed over the years, and we generally only see a dip in sales around Thanksgiving, when sweet potato pie's cousin, pumpkin pie, comes to town and people get a little tired of the whole family. This recipe calls for the sweet potatoes to be roasted in the oven as opposed to cooking them in boiling water. The roasting process will concentrate the rich sweetness of the potato and produce a much tastier filling.

**Yield: 1 (9½-inch) pie; serves 8**

2 cups cooked and puréed sweet potatoes (about 1¼ pounds uncooked)

3 large eggs

1 cup packed light brown sugar

1 cup heavy cream

2 tablespoons freshly squeezed orange juice

1 tablespoon orange zest

¼ cup (½ stick) unsalted butter, melted

½ teaspoon ground allspice

½ teaspoon freshly grated nutmeg

¼ teaspoon ground cinnamon

1 prebaked 9½-inch pie shell (page 260)

Whipped cream or vanilla ice cream, for serving

1. Preheat oven to 400°F.

2. Prick the sweet potatoes with a fork a few times and bake at 400°F for about an hour or until the potatoes are very soft. Remove the sweet potatoes from the oven and allow them to cool until you can handle them, then slice in half lengthwise and scrape the flesh out with a spoon. Purée the potato flesh in a food processor or press through a sieve. This step will ensure a smooth batter and result in a velvety finished product.

3. Lower the oven temperature to 350°F. Combine the sweet potato purée, eggs, brown sugar, cream, orange juice and zest, butter, and spices in a large bowl and blend together with a whisk or electric mixer. Pour the mixture into the prebaked pie shell.

4. Bake the pie at 350°F for 35 to 45 minutes. The timing can vary, depending on the depth of your pie shell. The center of the pie should be slightly wobbly when you remove it from the oven. Allow the pie to cool to room temperature before serving and serve with whipped cream or vanilla ice cream.

## Pecan Bread Pudding

Bread pudding is not only easy and satisfying, but it's a great way to use up leftover bread. You can use any type of bread, and if it's a little stale, all the better. You can omit the raisins, if you wish, but I think the little bit of fruity sweetness in the rich custard provides welcome contrast. Send this bread pudding over the top with a heavy drizzle of Bourbon Sauce.

¼ cup (½ stick) unsalted butter, at room temperature, divided

8 to 10 cups loosely packed cubed French bread (½-inch cubes)

6 large eggs

12 large egg yolks

2 cups heavy cream

4 cups milk

1 vanilla bean, split and scraped, or 2 teaspoons pure vanilla extract

2 cups sugar

1 teaspoon ground cinnamon

½ teaspoon freshly grated nutmeg

¾ cup golden raisins

1 cup pecan halves, slightly crushed

Bourbon Sauce (recipe follows)

1. Coat the bottom and sides of a 13 x 9 x 2-inch casserole pan with 2 tablespoons of the butter and spread the bread cubes evenly in the dish.

2. Combine the eggs and egg yolks, cream, milk, vanilla, sugar, cinnamon, and nutmeg in a large bowl and whisk until the sugar has dissolved.

3. Pour the custard over the bread and allow the mixture to soak for 30 minutes, pressing the bread cubes down every so often to help them absorb the custard. Scatter the remaining 2 tablespoons of butter, raisins, and the crushed pecans across the top of the bread pudding.

4. While the bread pudding is soaking, set a rack in the lower middle position of your oven and preheat oven to 325°F.

5. Place the dish containing the bread pudding into a larger casserole dish or roasting pan. It is important that the sides of the larger pan be at least as tall as the dish that contains the pudding. Fill the outer pan with enough water to come halfway up the sides of the inner pan and place in the oven.

6. Bake for about 1 hour or until a knife or skewer inserted in the middle of the pudding comes out clean. Carefully remove both pans from the oven, then remove the pan with the bread pudding from the water bath.

7. Serve warm or at room temperature with a heavy dousing of Bourbon Sauce.

## Bourbon Sauce

Yield: about ¾ cup

¼ cup (½ stick) unsalted butter

½ cup sugar

¼ cup bourbon

¼ heavy cream

Pinch of salt

1. Melt the butter over medium heat in small saucepot.

2. Add the remaining ingredients and bring to a simmer, whisking occasionally, until the sugar has dissolved and the sauce has thickened, about 3 minutes.

# Warm Chocolate Marquise

If you or someone you know is a chocolate freak, look no further—Valhalla is right in front of you. This is a variation of the classic chilled French dessert by the same name. I mean no disrespect to the original, but I think for a chocolate dessert to have the knockout punch it's capable of, it needs to be warm. Not quite a flourless chocolate cake yet not as light as a soufflé, this dessert lies somewhere in between, like a rich, warm pudding. It needs very little in the way of accompaniment: just a little bowl of lightly sweetened whipped cream on the side or a dollop of crème fraîche if you want a little tartness for contrast.

**Yield: 6 individual servings**

⅓ cup plus 1 tablespoon unsalted butter, divided

½ cup superfine sugar, divided

1 pound high-quality semisweet chocolate, chopped

4 large eggs at room temperature

Whipped cream or crème fraîche, for serving

1. Preheat oven to 300°F. Lightly coat the bottom and sides of six 8-ounce ramekins with 1 tablespoon of the butter. Pour ¼ cup of the superfine sugar into the first ramekin and gently roll the sugar around so that the bottom and sides are evenly coated. Pour the remaining sugar out of the first ramekin into the next dish and repeat until all the ramekins are coated with a thin layer of sugar.

2. Pour 2 to 3 inches of water into the bottom half of a double boiler, bring the water to a simmer over medium heat, and reduce the heat to low. Position the top of the double boiler over the hot water, making sure it isn't in direct contact with the water.

3. Place the remaining ⅓ cup of butter and the chocolate in the top portion of the double boiler and heat until they have melted. Stir or whisk gently to combine.

4. Using either a hand mixer or a stand mixer fitted with the whip attachment, whip the eggs and remaining ¼ cup of superfine sugar together on high speed in a medium-size bowl until they have doubled in volume.

5. With a rubber spatula, gently fold the egg mixture into the chocolate mixture in two or three batches until combined and uniform in color. Pour or spoon the mixture into the prepared ramekins to just below the rim.

6. Place the ramekins in a large casserole dish or roasting pan, which will function as a water bath. Place the casserole dish in the oven and carefully fill it with the water from a pitcher until the water comes halfway up the sides of the ramekins.

7. Bake for 45 to 60 minutes.

8. Carefully remove the water bath from the oven and then the ramekins from the water bath. Serve warm with whipped cream or crème fraîche.

# Pecan Pie

It's hard to beat a good piece of pecan pie. It's always been one of my favorites, but many pecan pies suffer from being too sweet or not having the right balance of other ingredients to pecans. I believe that if you are making pecan pie, it should first and foremost taste of pecans, with the remaining ingredients acting as a supporting cast. Over the years and through much trial and error, we have developed this recipe that delivers consistently balanced results. Most pecan pie recipes do not call for prebaking the pie shell, but I have found that prebaking helps to prevent the bottom of the crust from getting soggy.

**Yield: 1 (9- to 10-inch) pie; serves 8**

1 cup light brown sugar

⅔ cup light corn syrup

1 tablespoon dark rum

¼ cup (½ stick) unsalted butter

3 large eggs

1 teaspoon pure vanilla extract

2 cups broken pecan pieces

1 cup pecan halves

1 prebaked 9- to 10-inch pie shell (page 260)

Whipped cream or ice cream, for serving

1. Preheat oven to 350°F.

2. Combine the sugar, corn syrup, rum, and butter in a 2-quart saucepan. Heat the mixture over low heat to a gentle simmer, stirring occasionally, until you are sure that the sugar has dissolved, 1 to 2 minutes. Remove the pan from the heat and allow the mixture to cool for about 20 minutes. You want the syrup mixture to cool so that when you combine it with the eggs, they don't scramble.

3. Whisk the eggs in a medium-size bowl until creamy, then add the vanilla and broken pecan pieces. Combine the warm syrup mixture with the nut mixture and stir with a spoon or spatula until fully incorporated.

4. Pour the filling into a prebaked pie shell and top with the pecan halves. Bake for about 40 minutes. The center of the pie will be slightly wobbly when you take it out of the oven and will set as it cools. Serve the pie warm with whipped cream or ice cream.

# Key Lime Pie

A former sous chef, Greg Hoffman, brought this Key Lime Pie recipe to the table a few years back when we were reworking the dessert menu. Knowing that I have a strong aversion to almost any shortcut, it was only after I tried the pie and liked it that he told me it had no eggs and baked for less than 10 minutes. It's easy, fast, and good—what more could you want?

If you can't find fresh Key limes, look for Mexican limes. Both varieties are smaller and more yellowish than the dark green Persian limes found in most grocery stores. If you can't find Key or Mexican limes, don't worry and don't be tempted to buy the bottled Key lime juice that some helpful store clerk will probably suggest. Fresh juice from any lime is going to be infinitely better than bottled juice.

Even though this pie takes very little time to make, it does require several hours in the refrigerator, so factor that into your plan.

*(Continued)*

**Yield: 1 (9- to 10-inch) pie**

## *Graham cracker crust:*

2 cups graham cracker crumbs (from about 15 graham crackers)

½ cup sugar

½ cup (1 stick) unsalted butter, melted

## *Filling:*

3 cups sweetened condensed milk (about 2 [14-ounce] cans)

½ cup sour cream

¾ cup freshly squeezed Key lime juice (from about 16 limes)

2 tablespoons lime zest, divided

1. **Prepare the crust:** Preheat oven to 350°F.

2. Pulverize the graham crackers in a food processor. If you don't have a food processor or don't want to clean it, you can put the crackers in a resealable plastic bag and crush them with the back of a sauté pan or a rolling pin.

3. Place the graham cracker crumbs and sugar in a medium bowl and drizzle the melted butter over the crumbs while mixing with a wooden spoon or rubber spatula until the butter is fully incorporated. The mixture should look like coarse, wet sand.

4. Spread the graham cracker crumb mixture evenly into your pie dish, leaving a bit more on the outer edge so you have enough to go up the sides. Using a flat measuring cup for the bottom and your fingers or a spatula for the sides, firmly compact the crumb mixture to the bottom and sides of the pie dish.

5. Bake for 10 minutes. Remove from the oven and allow to cool while you make the filling.

6. **Prepare the filling:** Combine the sweetened condensed milk, sour cream, lime juice, and 1 tablespoon of the lime zest in a medium bowl and mix thoroughly.

7. Pour the mixture into your slightly cooled graham cracker crust and spread evenly with a rubber spatula.

8. Bake for 5 to 10 minutes. The pie should be slightly stiffer than when you placed it in the oven, but it might not be completely set. Look for tiny bubbles breaking on the surface of the pie. Remove the pie from the oven, allow to cool, and place in the refrigerator for at least 3 to 4 hours or up to overnight.

9. Garnish with the remaining tablespoon of lime zest.

# Crisps and Cobblers

It should be no surprise that Hattie's dessert menu gravitates toward folksy, home-style concoctions. In my mind, nothing characterizes this style of dessert more than the family of fruit crisps and cobblers. Although each of these desserts has a distinct identity, both contain fresh seasonal fruit topped with sweetened dough. Crisp fall apples, succulent spring stone fruits, or ripe summer berries provide seasonal variation to a dessert group than satisfies consistently year round. Crisps are generally more rustic than cobblers and are made by scattering a mixture of butter, sugar, flour, oats, and sometimes nuts in and around the fruit. Cobblers are made by arranging pieces of sweet biscuit dough on top of the fruit and baking it to form a crust. Both can be served warm or at room temperature, and depending on the fruit and personal taste, they can be paired with anything from a scoop of vanilla ice cream or whipped cream to a dollop of crème fraîche or just a drizzle of fresh cream.

## Apple Crisp

I am lucky to have spent a great deal of time in both of the two top apple-producing states in the country. And be it Washington State or Washington County, New York, fall is apple time. Starting in September, we will run apple crisp or cobbler straight through winter. Apples can vary greatly in their sweetness and texture, so I recommend mixing two or three varieties for the best results. While most apples respond well to baking, I would shy away from Red Delicious and Rome apples, as they tend to be watery and a bit mushy when baked.

NOTE: You can make extra topping and store it in an airtight container in the refrigerator for a month or more, so you can whip up this dessert on a whim.

**Yield: 6 to 8 servings**

## Apple filling:

3 to 4 pounds mixed apples, peeled, cored, and cut into ½-inch slices

½ teaspoon kosher salt

2 tablespoons sugar

¼ teaspoon ground cinnamon

¼ teaspoon freshly grated nutmeg

Juice and zest of 1 lemon

2 tablespoons brandy, triple sec, or water

3 tablespoons cornstarch

## Topping:

2 cups rolled oats

1 cup all-purpose flour

1 cup sugar

1 cup light brown sugar

1 cup (2 sticks) unsalted butter at room temperature

1. Preheat oven to 350°F.

2. **Prepare the apples:** Place the apple slices in a large bowl and add the remaining ingredients. Toss or stir the apple mixture gently until well combined. Let the fruit macerate while you make the topping, or for 20 minutes or so if you already have the topping made. Gently toss the mixture a few times to encourage the apples to give up some of their juice and begin to form a syrup.

3. **Prepare the topping:** Using a spoon, combine the oats, flour, sugar, and brown sugar in a medium-size bowl until the mixture is uniform in texture.

4. Pinch off marble-size pieces of the butter and scatter them evenly around the oat mixture. Work the butter into the oat mixture with your hands or a pastry cutter until the mixture holds together and looks crumbly.

5. Transfer the fruit to a 2-quart baking dish and crumble an even layer of the topping over the top of the apples.

6. Bake the crisp for 45 to 60 minutes or until the apples are cooked and the oat topping is crispy. If the topping begins browning before the apples are cooked, cover the top loosely with a piece of aluminum foil.

## Peach and Blueberry Cobbler

Hattie was known to make a mean peach cobbler. I can only hope that my version comes close to the original. You can experiment with the variety of stone fruit and berries to suit your taste. Nectarines and plums work well, and big, plump blackberries are always delicious and pair well with any stone fruit.

**Yield: 6 to 8 servings**

## Fruit:

5 pounds peaches, peeled, pitted, and cut into ½-inch slices (see note)

1 pint blueberries

½ teaspoon kosher salt

3 tablespoons sugar

¼ cup light brown sugar

Juice and zest of 1 lemon

2 tablespoons peach schnapps or triple sec

2 tablespoons cornstarch

## Biscuit dough:

2 cups all-purpose flour, plus more for dusting

⅓ cup sugar, plus 3 to 4 tablespoons, for dusting

½ teaspoon kosher salt

2 teaspoons baking powder

½ cup (1 stick) unsalted butter, chilled and cut into pea-size pieces

½ teaspoon pure vanilla extract

1¼ cups heavy cream, divided

1. **Prepare the fruit:** Combine the peach slices and the blueberries in a large bowl. Add the remaining ingredients and toss or stir with a spoon until well combined. Allow the fruit mixture to sit and macerate while you make the biscuit dough. Gently toss the mixture a few times to encourage the peaches to give up some of their juice and begin to form a syrup.

2. **Prepare the biscuit dough:** Preheat oven to 375°F.

3. Combine the dry ingredients in a medium-size bowl.

4. Using a pastry cutter or a fork, cut the chilled butter pieces into the dry mixture until the dough looks like crumbly cornmeal. It's OK if some lumps of butter remain. You don't want to overhandle biscuit dough, so if in doubt, less is more.

5. Combine the vanilla with 1 cup of the cream and slowly drizzle the cream over the dough mixture until the dough starts to come together. The finished dough should hold together and be moist but not sticky.

6. Turn out the dough onto a floured surface and gather it together to form a mounded disk. At this point, the dough can be wrapped and stored in the refrigerator if you aren't ready to assemble the cobbler.

7. On a floured surface, pat or roll the dough until it's about ¾-inch thick. Using a biscuit cutter, cut out as many rounds as you can. The first cutting of biscuit dough is always the best, so try to get the best yield you can by spacing the cuts as closely as possible. Re-form and reroll the scraps, if necessary.

8. Arrange the biscuits on top of the fruit so that the biscuits touch, but leave some fruit visible in the spaces in between. This will allow some of the fruit to bubble up between the biscuits, making for a beautiful crust.

*(Continued)*

9.    Brush the top of the biscuits with the reserved ¼ cup of cream and give them a generous sprinkle of sugar. Bake for 30 to 40 minutes, or until the biscuits are golden and the fruit is bubbly.

NOTE: Peel the peaches by immersing them a few at a time in a pot of boiling water for about 30 seconds, and then transfer them with a slotted spoon into a bowl of ice water. This step will cook the skin of the peach, but not the peach itself, and allow the skins to slip off easily.

# Hattie's cocktails

This collection of cocktails contains original drinks as well as our take on some classics. Like good cooking, a good cocktail is all about balance. Most cocktails contain very few ingredients; therefore, the proper ratio of ingredients makes the difference between a good cocktail and one that is either too sweet, too sour, or too strong. If you're going to keep a home bar stocked to the extent needed to make even the most basic cocktails, you should invest in the small amount of equipment needed to produce consistent results. Only about five items are necessary and they will cost you less than the price of a midrange bottle of bourbon. A basic setup would consist of a shaker, strainer, jigger, cocktail spoon, and muddler. I've suggested glasses that are traditionally used for certain drinks, but obviously almost any glass will do.

All these recipes are for a single drink, except for Hattie's Sangria, which serves 4 to 6. The bar at Hattie's, despite being seasonal and tucked in the back of an alley, is loved by locals, tourists, and industry professionals. Whether you call our bar the swamp, the Hatti-o, or the French Quarter lounge, it has become as much of an institution in its own way as the restaurant. In the end, it's as much about relaxing with friends and having a good time in a familiar and comfortable place as it is about the cocktail.

# Man-Hattie's

2 ounces honey bourbon (for example, Jim Beam Honey Bourbon)

½ ounce dark vermouth

2 to 3 dashes of Peychaud's Bitters

A fresh or preserved cherry, for garnish

1. Fill a martini or rocks glass with ice.

2. Fill a shaker with ice.

3. Add the bourbon, vermouth, and bitters to the shaker and shake vigorously.

4. Dump the ice from the martini glass and strain the drink into the chilled glass, or pour into the rocks glass.

5. Garnish with a cherry.

# Firewater Punch

2 ounces cherry moonshine
(for example, Junior Johnson's
Midnight Moon Cherry Moonshine)

1½ ounces freshly brewed iced
tea

¼ ounce freshly squeezed lemon
juice

¼ ounce simple syrup (page 235)

A fresh or preserved cherry, for
garnish

1. Fill a highball or mason jar with ice. (We serve this drink in a mason jar.)

2. Fill a shaker with ice.

3. Add the moonshine, iced tea, lemon juice, and simple syrup and shake vigorously.

4. Strain into the ice-filled highball glass.

5. Garnish with a cherry.

## Classic Daiquiri

2 ounces white rum (for example, Bacardi)

1 ounce freshly squeezed lime juice

½ ounce Simple Syrup (recipe follows)

Lime slice for garnish

1. Fill a martini glass with ice.

2. Fill a shaker with ice.

3. Add the rum, lime juice, and simple syrup to the shaker and shake vigorously.

4. Dump out the ice from the martini glass and strain the daiquiri into the chilled glass.

5. Garnish with the lime slice.

## Simple Syrup

**Yield: 2 cups**

2 cups sugar

1 cup water

1. In a small saucepan, bring the sugar and water to a boil; simmer until the sugar is dissolved, about 3 minutes. Remove from the heat and let cool completely.

2. Stored in an airtight container, simple syrup will last for months.

## Hattie's Sangria

1 bottle (750 ml) red wine

¼ cup brandy (E&J XO or Apple Jack)

¼ cup orange-flavored liqueur (triple sec or Grand Marnier)

2 tablespoons fresh lime juice

2 tablespoons fresh orange juice

½ orange, thinly sliced

½ lemon, thinly sliced

6 strawberries, quartered

1 apple, cored, and cut into thin wedges

1 bottle (20 ounce) ginger ale

Orange slice and a strawberry, for garnish

1. Combine all the ingredients except the ginger ale in a large sealable container.

2. Cover and chill completely for 1 to 2 hours.

3. When ready to serve, add the ginger ale to the wine mixture.

4. Fill a wine or highball glass with ice and pour in the Sangria.

5. Garnish with an orange slice and a strawberry.

**NOTE:** Berries, peaches or almost any seasonal fruit can be added. White wine can be substituted for red if you prefer.

# French Quarter Dark and Stormy

6 ounces ginger beer

½ ounce freshly squeezed lime juice

2 ounces dark rum (for example, Gosling or Myers's)

Lime wedge for garnish

1. Fill a highball glass with ice.

2. Add the ginger beer and lime juice.

3. Float the dark rum on top of the cocktail by carefully pouring the rum over the back of a bar spoon.

4. Garnish with the lime wedge.

# Mint Julep

3 to 4 mint leaves

2 ounces bourbon (for example, Woodford Reserve)

½ ounce simple syrup (page 235)

Fresh mint sprig for garnish

1.  Fill a julep cup (see note) or rocks glass halfway with ice and muddle the mint leaves with the ice.

2.  Fill the julep cup or glass the rest of the way with ice.

3.  Add the bourbon and simple syrup and stir.

4.  Garnish with the mint sprig.

**NOTE:** Traditionally a mint julep is served in a small tapered silver cup, which gives the cocktail a classic elegance.

# Hattie's Mojito

6 mint leaves

2 ounces white rum (for example, Bacardi Silver)

1 ounce Simple Syrup (page 235)

½ ounce freshly squeezed lime juice

Splash of club soda

Lime wedge, mint sprig, and a sugarcane swizzle stick (available online) for garnish

1. Fill the shaker one-third of the way with ice.

2. Add the mint leaves and muddle (see note).

3. Fill the shaker the rest of the way with ice and add the rum, simple syrup, and lime juice.

4. Vigorously shake, then pour into a highball glass.

5. Add the club soda.

6. Garnish with the lime wedge, mint sprig, and sugarcane swizzle stick.

**NOTE:** You can add fresh seasonal fruit to the muddle stage, if you wish. At Hattie's we often use mangoes, pineapples, or whatever berries are available at our local farmers' market.

# Back Porch Lemonade

2 ounces raspberry vodka (for example, Stoli Razberi)

6 ounces Fresh Lemonade (recipe follows)

Fresh raspberries and a lemon wedge for garnish

1. Fill a highball glass with ice.

2. Add the raspberry vodka and lemonade.

3. Garnish with the raspberries and lemon wedge.

## Fresh Lemonade

1 cup freshly squeezed lemon juice (about 6 lemons)

½ to ¾ cup superfine sugar

4 cups water

1. Combine the lemon juice, ½ cup sugar, and the water and stir vigorously until the sugar has dissolved.

2. Taste the lemonade and add more sugar, if necessary. You want a pleasant balance of tart and sweet.

## Cool as a Cucumber

3 cucumber slices

1½ ounces gin (for example, Hendrick's)

¾ ounce elderflower liqueur (for example, St-Germain)

¼ ounce freshly squeezed lime juice

Splash of tonic

Cucumber slice for garnish

1. Fill a shaker one-third of the way with ice.

2. Add the three cucumber slices and muddle.

3. Fill the shaker the rest of the way with ice.

4. Add the gin, elderflower liqueur, and lime juice and shake vigorously.

5. Pour unstrained into a highball glass.

6. Add the tonic and garnish with the cucumber slice.

2 ounces vodka (for example, Ketel One)

4 ounces tomato juice

1 tablespoon prepared horseradish

1 teaspoon finely chopped garlic

1 teaspoon freshly squeezed lemon juice

1 teaspoon freshly squeezed lime juice

2 dashes Worcestershire sauce

2 dashes Hattie's Hot Sauce or other Louisiana-style hot sauce

Pinch of freshly ground black pepper

Pinch of celery salt

Celery stalk, green olives, and lemon wedges, for garnish

# Bloody Mary

1. Fill a pint glass with ice.

2. Fill a shaker one-third of the way with ice.

3. Add all the ingredients, except the garnishes, and shake vigorously.

4. Strain into the ice-filled glass.

5. Garnish with the celery stalk, green olives, and lemon wedges.

# Hot Toddy

2 ounces bourbon (for example, Maker's Mark Reserve)

1 lemon slice

½ ounce honey

Hot water

Cinnamon stick for garnish

1.  Pour the bourbon into a brandy snifter.

2.  Add the lemon slice, honey, and enough hot water to fill the snifter. Stir.

3.  Garnish with the cinnamon stick.

# Hard Sweet Tea

2 ounces bourbon (for example, Maker's Mark)

3 ounces iced tea

1 ounce Simple Syrup (page 235)

Lemon wedge and a thyme sprig for garnish

1.  Fill a highball glass with ice.

2.  Fill a shaker full of ice.

3.  Add the bourbon, iced tea, and simple syrup to the shaker and shake vigorously.

4.  Strain into the ice-filled highball glass.

5.  Garnish with the lemon wedge and thyme sprig.

# Sazerac

¼ ounce Pernod

3 dashes Peychaud's Bitters

2 ounces bourbon (for example, Woodford Reserve)

¼ ounce Simple Syrup (page 235)

Lemon peel for garnish

1. Pour the Pernod into an empty rocks glass and tilt and twist the glass to coat the bottom and sides.

2. Fill the glass with ice.

3. Add the bitters, bourbon, and simple syrup and stir.

4. Garnish with the lemon peel.

# Pain Killer

2 ounces white rum (for example, Bacardi Silver)

4 ounces pineapple juice

1 ounce cream of coconut (for example, Coco López)

Orange wedge, preserved cherry, and freshly grated nutmeg (see note) for garnish

1.  Fill a shaker with ice.

2.  Add the rum, pineapple juice, and cream of coconut and shake well.

3.  Pour into a highball glass and garnish with the orange wedge, cherry, and nutmeg.

**NOTE:** It might sound like a strange ingredient for a cocktail, but the freshly grated nutmeg is the key to this cocktail. The drink will not be the same without it.

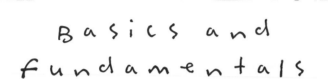

# Basics and fundamentals

# Notes on Frying at Home

One of the most frequent compliments we get about the fried chicken at Hattie's is that it's light, crisp, and never greasy. How do we do it? The answer is simple: high-quality, clean oil and maintaining the proper frying temperature. But achieving this in the home setting can be kind of tricky. Following a few general principles ensures that it can be done safely and effectively.

If you are cooking anything on the stove in oil, in essence you are frying. The difference between sautéing, panfrying, and deep-frying is the amount of oil in the pan. With sautéing, there is just enough oil in the pan to provide a medium for the heat to transfer to the food you are cooking. When you panfry an item, the oil will cover roughly one-third to half of the food you are cooking. With deep-frying, the amount of oil should be sufficient to fully submerge the food you are cooking. If you are going to deep-fry at home, accept the fact that you're going to need to purchase, clean, and store more oil than you may normally keep in your pantry. (More about that later.)

Good sautéing and panfrying results can be achieved with almost any heavy-gauge pan, provided that the pan and oil are hot, the item you are cooking is dry, and you don't crowd your pan. When it comes to deep-frying, there are a few more things to consider.

Three types of frying setups work well for deep-frying at home. The first and easiest method, but not the cheapest, is to purchase a tabletop fryer designed for the home cook. Sizes and quality vary, and with table-top fryers, you get what you pay for. You want to think about how much frying you're going to do and what you're going to fry, then purchase the largest model that best suits your needs and budget. Anytime you place food in the fryer, the temperature of the oil will drop. How quickly the fryer returns to its set temperature is the recovery time. Bigger is better for two reasons. First, a larger fryer is generally going to require a more powerful heating element, and second, the increased volume of hot oil will decrease the temperature drop and hence will shorten the recovery time. Tabletop fryers are good for both large and small items, are easy to operate, relatively easy to clean, and definitely the safest method.

The second method is an electric skillet. It is a great option for smaller to medium-size items. I like them because they are cheap, controlled by a thermostat, and provide powerful heat without an open flame—a big safety factor. The drawback is that generally electric skillets are not deep enough to deep-fry larger items.

The third method is the one your grandmother used, the old-school Dutch oven. Dutch ovens are typically made from cast iron, which is heavy, stable, and a great heat conductor, but a heavy-gauge steel or aluminum pot will also work. Although they are low tech, Dutch ovens make excellent and affordable stovetop fryers. Even some of the most upscale restaurants I've cooked in have used a stovetop Dutch oven for a fryer at times.

However, it's precisely because they are so low tech that they require more attention to detail than the other methods. In general, you will want to choose the biggest, heaviest pot you have. Temper this rule with some common sense—you don't need a 12-quart Dutch oven full of oil to fry half a dozen hushpuppies.

You definitely will need a candy thermometer or probe thermometer that will register temperatures up to at least 400°F. Keep a close eye on the temperature of your oil. You will be frying at temperatures between 325° and 350°F. Any lower and you're not really frying, while temperatures in excess of 400°F can be a fire hazard.

Do not fill the Dutch oven more than halfway with oil. When you place food items in the Dutch oven, they will displace that same amount of oil. If you have too much oil in the pot or try to fry too many items at once, the oil could overflow and start a nasty grease fire. That's how houses burn down.

Place the Dutch oven on the stove, fill it halfway with oil, and heat the oil over medium-high heat until it reaches 325°F. Then, lower the heat source enough to just maintain that temperature. As you begin to fry, you're going to need to adjust your heat up and down according to the oil temperature and how many items you are frying. The goal is to maintain 325° to 350°F throughout the frying process.

Make sure you set up your tabletop fryer, electric skillet, or Dutch oven away from any water. Hot oil and water are not friends. Even a few drops will splatter and pop, and a few tablespoons could be enough to make the fryer boil over, so make sure the items you're frying are dry. If you're frying a battered item, the flour in the batter will contain the moisture, and therefore the splatter also will be contained.

Never drop food into a hot fryer; instead, slip it into the oil as close to the surface of the oil as possible. If you drop food into the fryer from even a few inches above the surface it will splash hot oil everywhere, most likely including your hand and arm.

Regardless of which method you choose, you need to have a way to scoop the fried products out of the fryer. Even if you use a table-top fryer, the basket might not always be the best choice. A pair of tongs or a slotted spoon will work for some things, but I recommend a small spider or strainer, preferably with a wooden handle so it stays cool. You will also need a place for your food to rest once it's fried. A wire cooling rack or a cookie sheet lined with paper towels both work fine. It's important to season fried items immediately after cooking them, while they are still glistening with oil, so that the salt and pepper will stick.

To store used oil, all you need is a fine-mesh strainer and a container that can be sealed. You should be able to get many uses out of the oil before it's past its prime, provided you strain out the leftover food particles. If it smells rancid or burnt it's time to pitch it. The oil does not have to be refrigerated, but if you have the space, it will last longer under refrigeration. Some oils solidify or change color when they're cold, and that's fine.

Finally, get a small fire extinguisher. If you're careful, it's very unlikely that you will cause a fire, but it's always possible. Ask for one that's rated for a kitchen grease fire. The last thing you want to do is grab a water-filled fire extinguisher for a grease fire. In professional kitchens, it is inevitable that you're going to deal with small fires on occasion. I have seen smart, quick-thinking, battle-hardened cooks who are afraid of nothing be reduced to babbling idiots in the presence of a small fire, so don't make any assumptions about how you would react. Get a fire extinguisher, keep it close, and if you have to, use it.

# Making Stocks

The importance of flavorful, well-made stocks is one of the first things you learn in culinary school. It is simply a fundamental building block of great flavor and a necessary component in countless dishes. Preparing your own stocks will, without question, enhance the quality of any dish that calls for a particular stock. I encourage you to try the difference and see for yourself. While it does require some extra time and preparation, most of the work is passive and it can be done well in advance and stored in the freezer so you have it ready when needed.

Now, I know that despite all this encouragement and the irrefutable quality difference, not everybody is going to make their own stock. Heck, if I didn't have a restaurant where I have various stocks working all the time, I wouldn't make a stock every time I needed a cup or two.

If you use store-bought substitutions, choose wisely. Remember that the most expensive is not always the best, and go with lower-sodium varieties whenever you can.

If you are going to make your own, keep in mind these guiding principles:

Always use good, fresh ingredients. If you use bones, make sure you buy them fresh. In the case of chicken stock, it's economical to buy whole chickens, cut them up yourself, and freeze the bony pieces (backs and necks) until you have enough for making stock. Alternatively, you can just buy a stewing chicken and figure your excellent stock will justify the extra expense.

Fish or shellfish should smell of the ocean, with no hint of iodine or ammonia.

Use good-quality vegetables. Your stock is not the way to salvage the remnants of your vegetable drawer. Always start with cold water and allow the stock to come to a gentle simmer. Never boil stock. Skim and discard any fat, scum, or foam that rises to the top throughout the cooking process. Simmer all stocks as slowly as your stove will allow.

You can reduce meat stocks, to concentrate the flavor and reduce the space required in your refrigerator or freezer. However, be careful when reducing fish or shellfish stocks, as they can get too strong, and vegetable stocks will lose flavor if reduced. There are entire books devoted to the subject of making stocks, their uses, and their derivative sauces, but these are the broad strokes and will keep you out of trouble.

**Yield: about 2 gallons stock**

5 pounds bony chicken pieces, or 1 (4- to 5-pound) stewing chicken

1 pound onions, chopped

½ pound carrots, peeled and chopped

5 celery ribs, chopped

1 garlic bulb, halved

4 bay leaves

5 black peppercorns

5 sprigs fresh thyme

5 sprigs fresh parsley

1 sprig fresh rosemary

2½ gallons cold water

# Chicken Stock

1. Rinse the chicken thoroughly and trim off any excess fat.

2. Place all the ingredients in a 12-quart stockpot filled with cold water and bring to a gentle simmer over medium-low heat. Simmer for 5 to 6 hours while skimming off any fat or scum that rises to the surface.

3. Strain and discard all solids (including the sacrificial stewing chicken, if used). Use or cool completely and store in the refrigerator or freezer.

# Vegetable Stock

**Yield: about 1 gallon stock**

1 pound onions, chopped

2 leeks, white part only, cleaned and chopped

2 carrots, peeled and chopped

2 parsnips, peeled and chopped

3 celery ribs, chopped

1 celery root, peeled and chopped (optional)

1 fennel bulb, chopped

2 tomatoes, chopped

1 garlic bulb, halved

4 bay leaves

5 black peppercorns

5 sprigs fresh thyme

5 sprigs fresh parsley

1 sprig fresh rosemary

1½ gallons cold water

1. Place all the ingredients in an 8-quart stockpot and bring to a gentle simmer over medium heat. Simmer for 1 hour while skimming off the foam that rises to the surface.

2. Strain, discard all solids, and use, or cool completely and store in the refrigerator or freezer.

# Fish Stock

**Yield: about 1 gallon stock**

¼ cup olive oil

1 onion, chopped

2 leeks, white and green parts, cleaned and chopped

2 parsnips, peeled and chopped

3 celery ribs, chopped

1 fennel bulb, chopped

6 pounds fish bones

4 bay leaves

5 black peppercorns

5 sprigs fresh thyme

5 sprigs fresh parsley

2 cups white wine

1 gallon cold water

1.  Heat the olive oil in an 8-quart stockpot over medium heat. Add all the vegetables and sauté for 5 minutes or until the vegetables begin to soften.

2.  While the vegetables are cooking, rinse the fish bones well under cold water and drain in a colander.

3.  Place the fish bones on top of the vegetables and add the bay leaves, peppercorns, herbs, wine, and water.

4.  Bring the stock to a gentle simmer over medium-low heat. Simmer for 35 to 45 minutes while skimming off any foam or scum that rises to the surface.

5.  Strain, discard the solids, and use, or cool completely and store in the refrigerator or freezer.

# Shellfish Stock

**Yield: about 1 gallon stock**

6 pounds chopped shrimp, crab, and/or lobster shells

¼ cup olive oil

1 onion, chopped

2 leeks, white and green parts, chopped

2 carrots, peeled and chopped

3 celery ribs, chopped

1 fennel bulb, chopped

3 ounces tomato paste

4 bay leaves

5 black peppercorns

5 sprigs fresh thyme

5 sprigs fresh parsley

2 cups white wine

1 gallon cold water

1. Rinse the chopped shells well under cold water and drain in a colander. Heat the oil in a 12-quart stockpot over medium heat.

2. Add the shells and sauté for 5 minutes. Add the vegetables and cook for about 20 minutes, or until the vegetables begin to turn brown and caramelize. Add the tomato paste and cook for another 5 minutes.

3. Add the bay leaves, peppercorns, herbs, wine, and water and bring to a gentle simmer over medium heat. Simmer for 35 to 45 minutes while skimming off any foam or scum that rises to the surface.

4. Strain, discard the solids, and use, or cool completely and store in the refrigerator or freezer.

# Basic Recipe for Cooking Dried Beans

1. Cover the beans with cold water and allow to soak for 12 to 24 hours. Alternatively, you can quick-soak the beans by bringing the beans and water to a boil and then turning off the heat and allowing the beans to sit for 1 hour. Whichever method you choose, once the beans have soaked, strain off the soaking water and begin the cooking process with fresh water or stock.

2. In a 4- to 6-quart stockpot, combine the beans, water or stock, onion, celery, carrot, garlic, bay leaves, and salt.

3. Over high heat, bring the beans to a simmer. Lower the heat to medium-low and continue to cook, stirring occasionally. It is essential that the beans remain covered with about an inch of liquid, and it is likely that you will need to add liquid during the cooking process. Beans, like pasta, like room to swim around while cooking, but they like to swim slowly. Resist the urge to blast them with heat to speed things up—they'll break apart. The time it takes to cook a pound of beans will vary depending on the type and size of the beans, but figure at least 1 to 2 hours. When beans are cooked properly, they are creamy and tender with no hint of crunch or grittiness.

**Yield: 6 cups cooked beans**

1 pound dried beans

8 cups water or stock, plus more as needed

1 onion, quartered

1 celery rib

1 carrot, peeled

3 whole garlic cloves

2 bay leaves

1 tablespoon salt

# Pie Dough

**Yield: 1 (9- to 10-inch) pie crust**

2½ cups all-purpose flour

1 teaspoon kosher salt

1 teaspoon sugar

½ cup (1 stick) unsalted butter, chilled

½ cup vegetable shortening, chilled

6 tablespoons cold water

1. Place the flour, salt, and sugar in a food processor and pulse a few times to combine.

2. Add the cold butter and shortening and pulse until the mixture looks like coarse cornmeal.

3. Slowly add the water until the mixture just starts to come together. Stop adding water long before a dough ball actually forms. If the flour mixture sticks together when you squeeze it in your hand, as opposed to crumbling apart, you have enough water in the dough. You might not need the entire 6 tablespoons of water, so if it looks right and you have not used all the water, that's fine.

4. Turn out the dough onto a work surface and gather it together with your hand, pressing and flattening it until it is ¼ to ½ inch thick.

5. Wrap the dough in plastic wrap and put it in the refrigerator for at least an hour while you prepare the filling or fillings.

## Prebaking a Pie Shell

Once you have rolled and formed your piecrust, preheat oven to 375°F. Prick the bottom and sides of the pie dough with a fork. Line the dough with foil or parchment paper and fill with pie weights or dried beans. Bake the pie shell for 15 to 20 minutes, or until the dough is starting to change color.

# Rice

On my first day of culinary school, I learned a valuable lesson concerning rice: All rice has a specific ratio of liquid to rice that is needed for the rice to cook properly. You can either spend the time memorizing how the ratios differ from white rice to brown rice to wild rice, or you can just read the side of the package that it came in and get on with it. I recommend Plan B.

# Sources

## NEWSPAPER ARTICLES

Evans, John. "Hattie dies but memories and Chicken Shack remain." *The Saratogian*, 24 April 1998.

McKnight, Doug. "A Slice of the South." *The Saratogian,* 18 October 1987.

Schwartz, Elizabeth S. "Diners have a taste of Hattie's meals." *The Saratogian*, 30 July 1989.

Sisario, Ben. "Folk Music Heaven, Upstairs." *The New York Times*, 23 October 2013.

Wing, Jill. "Million Dollar Lady benefit planned in memory of Hattie Austin." *The Saratogian*, 26 August 2001.

## BOOKS

Bolster, George. *George Bolster's Saratoga Springs*. Norfolk, VA: Donning Co., 1990.

Bucciferro, Harry. *Saratoga 150: Celebrating 150 Years of Racing in Saratoga*. Albany, NY: Saratoga Living LLC, 2013.

Holmes, Timothy. *Saratoga Spring, New York: a Brief History*. Charleston, SC: The History Press, 2008.

Joki, Robert. *Saratoga Lost: Images of Victorian America*. Hesenville, NY: Black Dome Press, 1998.

Spiegel, Ted. *Saratoga, the Place and Its People*. New York: H. N. Abrams, 1988.

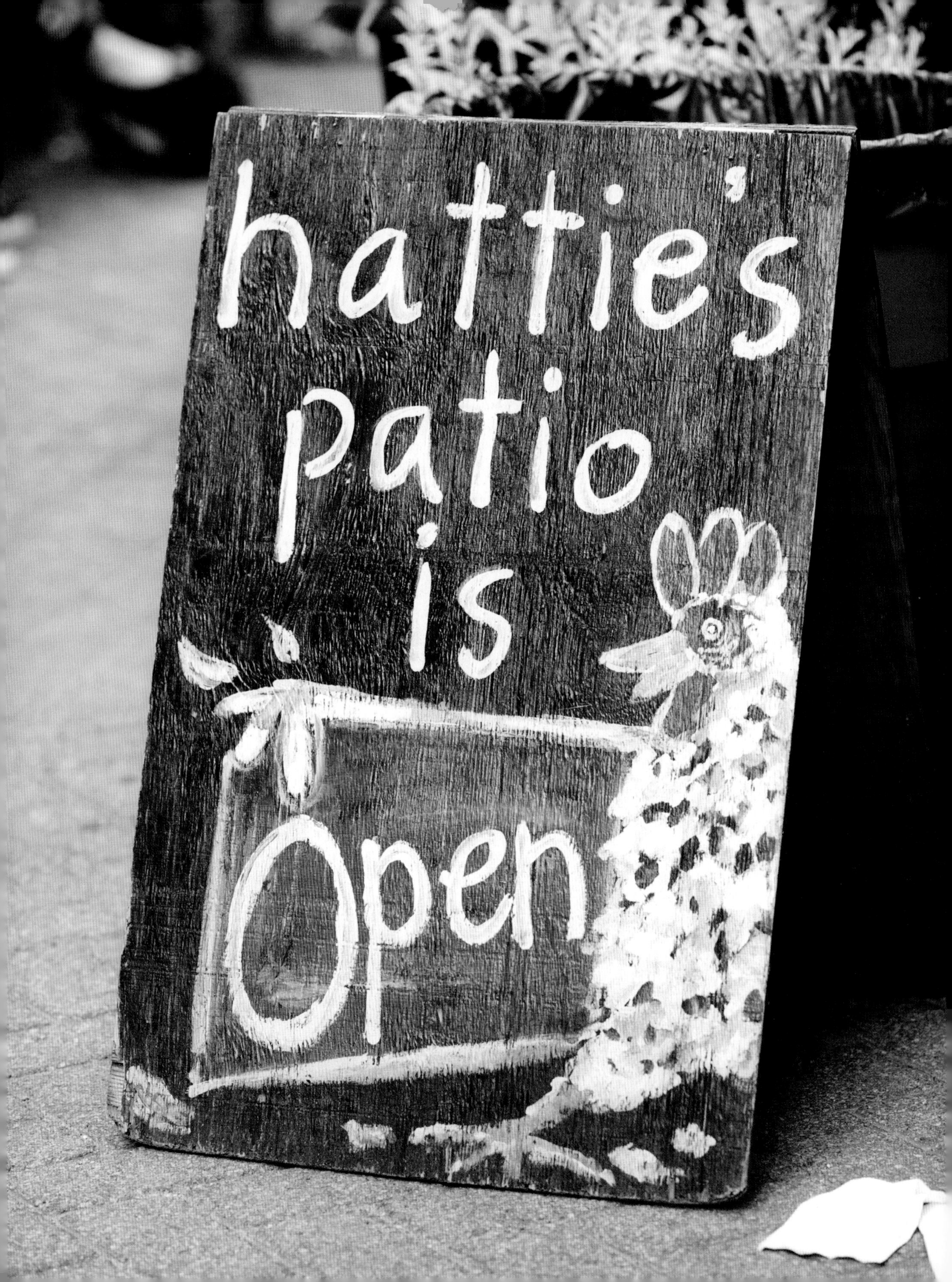
hattie's
patio
is
Open

# acknowledgments

I'm not sure when I began to show an interest in cooking, but as the only child of two busy working parents, I'm sure it was in part self-preservation. As the story goes, my parents stopped hiring baby sitters when they realized that I was cooking for them.

My parents, without agenda, began my food education with exposure that ranged from neighborhood garden co-operatives to high-caliber restaurants. My Aunt Joan and Uncle David, who have been a second set of parents, had a catering business for a few years and began a gourmet club that has met continuously since the late 1970s. My Aunt Lynn and Uncle Neil graciously allowed me to live with their family in Manhattan so I could afford to work at some of the city's finest restaurants. The collective food experiences my family shared had a strong impact and I now find myself, years later, somewhere near the middle of a career as a professional chef and restaurateur.

Many people, most significantly my wife Beth, have pushed me toward writing a cookbook. The ante was raised significantly after gaining national attention on Food Network's *Throwdown with Bobby Flay* and most everyone, Beth leading the charge, thought I should crank out a book to capitalize on the moment. It was sound advice that, much to the irritation of Beth, I ignored. A few years later, Scott Mendel, a customer and book agent by trade approached me about writing a cookbook while visiting his daughter at Skidmore College. Scott's daughter graduated before I could be convinced to actually write the proposal, but eventually I delivered. Beth and Scott can and should claim victory and I thank them for their persistence and patience.

The actual writing of the book has been an interesting experience to say the least. I have enjoyed it and hated it, and, like most good things, it has come with some sacrifice. Much of that sacrifice has come at the expense of my children and staff who have had to endure my absence. Kids need their dad and a ship needs its captain. I would like to thank Zoe, Charlie, and the entire Hattie's staff for putting up with the process.

Writing a cookbook is, by nature, a collaborative process. I would like to thank Aunt Joan and Uncle David, John DePrez, Christine Goforth, Anne Winter, Leslie Pendleton, and my mother for serving as recipe testers and providing their valuable feedback. Heather Bohm-Tallman, for her wonderful photos and commitment to the project. Michael L. Noonan, Mary Ann Lynch, Fred Mckinney, and the Saratoga Springs History Museum for providing historical photos. I am also grateful for the expertise of the editors and staff at The Countryman Press who turned a bunch of manuscript pages and photos into a book.

Most important, I would like to thank my mother and father for supporting me when, after graduating college, I explained that I wanted to cook for a living. Specific to this project, I want to thank them for teaching me how to write. Growing up with two editors as parents led to lots of red ink on anything I wrote from middle school through college. But I learned, and as a result, when Scott asked if I could write, I could confidently say, "Maybe, uhh, well, uhh, I think so. "

My father would be proud and I wish he could have seen this book. My mother has been looking at it off and on for a couple of years and has helped edit at every stage. I am grateful for her energy and skill. It is rare that a mother and son get the opportunity to share a project that caters to their own unique talents while being centered on a shared passion. For that experience alone, this process has been something I will cherish forever.

# index

## A

Aioli, Scallion, 154
American cheese, in The World's Best
    Egg Sandwich, 194–96
andouille (sausage)
    Andouille, Caramelized Onion, and
        Cheddar Omelet, 202–3
    Andouille Pigs in a Blanket, 38–39
    and Cheddar-Stuffed Mushrooms,
        57–58
    and Pimento Cheese Sliders, 136–37
    Shrimp, Andouille, and Corn
        Gumbo, 88–89
appetizers. *See* starters, nibbles, and
    noshes
Apple cider brine, 131
Apple Crisp, 213–14
Austin, Hattie Moseley, 14–16
avocados, in The World's Best Egg
    Sandwich, 194–96

## B

bacon
    caramelized, in The World's Best
        Egg Sandwich, 194–96
    Caramelized Onion and Bacon Tart,
        35–37
    Caramelized Onions and Bacon,
        Chicken Livers with, 59–61
    in Dirty Rice, 180–81
    Hattie's Meat Loaf, 150–51
    Salmon with Savoy Cabbage,
        Caramelized Pearl Onions, and,
        109–10
    Tomato Bacon Jam, 97
    Warm Chicken, Bacon, and
        Arugula Salad, 142–43
Baked Beans, Creole, 165–67

Baking Powder Dumplings, 78
basics and fundamentals, 28, 245–59
    Brown Veal Stock, 252–53
    Chicken Stock, 251
    cooking dried beans, 257
    cooking rice, 259
    equipment for frying, 248
    Fish Stock, 255
    frying at home, 246–48
    making stocks, 249–50
    Pie Dough, 258
    Shellfish Stock, 256
    Vegetable Stock, 254
BBQ sauce, in Ribs Without a Smoker,
    147–49
BBQ Shrimp, Savory, 49–50
beans and legumes
    black-eyed peas, in Hoppin' John
        Salad, 190–91
    dried, cooking, 257
    dried, in Creole Baked Beans,
        165–67
    dried, in Red Beans and Rice, 74–75
beef
    Andouille and Pimento Cheese
        Sliders, 136–37
    Blackened Skirt Steak with Crispy
        Blue Cheese Grit Cakes and
        Smoked Tomato Butter, 138–41
    Brisket Chili, 66–68
    Chicken-Fried Steak, 144–46
    Hattie's Meat Loaf, 150–51
    Pot Roast, 132–35
beer, in Brisket Chili, 66–68
Beignets, 197–98
bell peppers, in Sweet Corn Relish, 53
Biscuits, 168–69
Biscuits and Sausage Gravy, 204–5

Blackened Skirt Steak with Crispy Blue
    Cheese Grit Cakes and Smoked
    Tomato Butter, 138–41
Bloody Mary, 240
blueberries, in Peach and Blueberry
    Cobbler, 215–17
blue cheese
    Blue Cheese Grit Cakes, 140–41
    Pecan Blue Cheese Dressing, 45
bourbon cocktails
    Hard Sweet Tea, 242
    Hot Toddy, 25
    Man-Hattie's, 231
    Mint Julep, 236
    Sazerac, 243
Bourbon Sauce, 221
brandy, in Hattie's Sangria, 234
Bread, English Muffin, 196
bread puddings
    Pecan Bread Pudding, 220–21
    Savory Corn Bread Pudding,
        188–89
breakfast and brunch, 193–209
    Andouille, Caramelized Onion, and
        Cheddar Omelet, 202–3
    Beignets, 197–98
    Biscuits and Sausage Gravy, 204–5
    Buttermilk Pancakes and Waffles,
        206–7
    English Muffin Bread, 196
    Pain Perdu, 208–9
    Two Potato Ham Hash, 200–201
    The World's Best Egg Sandwich,
        194–96
Brisket Chili, 66–68
Brown Butter Balsamic Vinaigrette,
    105
Brown Butter Lemon Vinaigrette, 113

brunch. *See* breakfast and brunch
Buttermilk Dressing, 48
Buttermilk Pancakes and Waffles, 206–7

## C

cabbage
    in coleslaws, 108, 175, 178–79
    Savoy Cabbage, Caramelized Pearl
        Onions, and Bacon, Salmon
        with, 109–10
Cajun Coleslaw
    with Brown Butter Lemon
        Vinaigrette, Panfried Softshell
        Crab over, 111–13
    recipe for, 175
capers, in Tartar Sauce, 94
Caramelized Bacon, 195
Caramelized Onion, and Cheddar
    Omelet, Andouille, 202–3
Caramelized Onion and Bacon Tart,
    35–37
Catfish, Fried with Tartar Sauce Two
    Ways, 92–94
cheddar cheese
    Andouille, Caramelized Onion, and
        Cheddar Omelet, 202–3
    Andouille and Cheddar-Stuffed
        Mushrooms, 57–58
    Cheese Straws, 40–42
    Macaroni and Cheese, 71–73
    Pimento Cheese, 62–63
cheese. *See* American cheese; blue
    cheese; cheddar cheese
Cheese Straws, 40–42
cherry moonshine, in Firewater Punch,
    232
chicken
    Chicken and Dumplings, 76–78
    Chicken Stock, 251
    The Fried Chicken, 155–57
    Good and Evil Chicken Wings,
        43–45
    Jambalaya, 81–83
    Jerk Chicken with tropical Fruit
        Salsa and Scallion Aioli, 152–54
    livers, in Dirty Rice, 180–81
    Livers with Caramelized Onions
        and Bacon, 59–61
    Warm Chicken, Bacon, and
        Arugula Salad, 142–43

Chicken-Fried Steak, 144–46
Chicken Livers with Caramelized
    Onions and Bacon, 59–61
Chili, Brisket, 66–68
chili peppers
    in Brisket Chili, 66–68
    in Jerk Paste, 153
    poblano, in Two Potato Ham Hash,
        200–201
    serrano, in Cilantro Chutney, 108
Chocolate Marquise, Warm, 222–23
chorizo sausage
    Monkfish with Clams and Chorizo,
        125–27
    in Stone Soup, 86–87
Chutney, Cilantro, 108
cilantro, in Tropical Fruit Salsa, 154
Cilantro Chutney, 108
Clams, Steamed, with Saffron, Tomato,
    and Thyme, 69–70
Clams and Chorizo, Monkfish with,
    125–27
cobblers and crisps, 212–17
cocktails (Hattie's), 229–44
    Back Porch Lemonade, 238
    Bloody Mary, 240
    Classic Daiquiri, 233
    Cool as a Cucumber, 239
    Firewater Punch, 232
    French Quarter Dark and Stormy, 235
    Fresh Lemonade, 238
    Hard Sweet Tea, 242
    Hattie's Mojito, 237
    Hattie's Sangria, 234
    Hot Toddy, 241
    Man-Hattie's, 231
    Mint Julep, 236
    Pain Killer, 244
    Sazerac, 243
Cod, Prosciutto-Wrapped, with
    Vegetables Provençal, 114–15
coleslaw
    Cajun, 175
    Cranberry, 178–79
    Napa Cabbage Slaw, 108
Collard Greens, 182–83
Cool as a Cucumber, 239
corn
    Basic Grits, 173–74
    Corn Bread, 176–77

    in Crawfish Boil, 98–101
    Creamy Hominy, 160–61
    in Hoppin' John Salad, 190–91
    in Hush Puppies with Honey Butter,
        32–34
    Savory Corn Bread Pudding, 188–89
    Shrimp, Andouille, and Corn
        Gumbo, 88–89
    Sweet Corn Relish, 53
Crab, Panfried Softshell, over Cajun
    Coleslaw with Brown Butter
    Lemon Vinaigrette, 111–13
Crab Cakes with Sweet Corn Relish
    and Lime Mayo, 51–53
Cranberry Coleslaw, 178–79
crawfish
    Crawfish Boil, 98–101
    Crawfish Étouffée, 79–80
    how to eat, 101
cream of coconut, in Pain Killer, 244
Creole Baked Beans, 165–67
Creole Tartar Sauce, 94
crisps and cobblers, 212–17
cucumbers
    Cool as a Cucumber, 239
    Cucumber Salad, 186–87
    in Gazpacho, 84–85

## D

Daiquiri, Classic, 233
Dark and Stormy, French Quarter, 235
desserts, 211–28
    Apple Crisp, 213–14
    fruit crisps and cobblers, 212
    Key Lime Pie, 226–28
    Peach and Blueberry Cobbler, 215–17
    Pecan Bread Pudding, 220–21
    Pecan Pie, 224–25
    Sweet Potato Pie, 218–19
    Warm Chocolate Marquise, 222–23
Deviled Eggs, 54–56
Dirty Rice, 180–81
doughnuts (Beignets), 197–98
Dry Rub, 149
Dumplings, Baking Powder, 78

## E

earth and air. *See* beef; chicken; pork
eggs
    in bread puddings, 188–89, 220–21

Deviled Eggs, 54–56
Egg Sandwich, The World's Best, 194–96
Omelet, Andouille, Caramelized Onion, and Cheddar, 202–3
English Muffin Bread, 196
equipment, 27–28, 248
Étouffée, Crawfish, 79–80

F

fennel, in Chicken and Dumplings, 76–78
final temptations. See desserts
Firewater Punch, 232
fish and seafood, 91–119, 122–27
    Catfish, Fried, with Tartar Sauce Two Ways, 92–94
    Clams, Steamed, with Saffron, Tomato, and Thyme, 69–70
    Cod, Prosciutto-Wrapped, with Vegetables Provençal, 114–15
    Crab, Panfried Softshell, over Cajun Coleslaw with Brown Butter Lemon Vinaigrette, 111–13
    Crab Cakes with Sweet Corn Relish and Lime Mayo, 51–53
    crawfish, how to eat, 101
    Crawfish Boil, 98–101
    Crawfish Étouffée, 79–80
    Halibut with Wilted Spinach, Roasted Shiitakes, and Mushroom Nage, 116–19
    Monkfish with Clams and Chorizo, 125–27
    Oysters, Fried, with Napa Cabbage Slaw and Cilantro Chutney, 106–8
    Salmon with Savoy Cabbage, Caramelized Pearl Onions, and Bacon, 109–10
    Sea Scallops, Seared, with Grits, Watercress, and Brown Butter Balsamic Vinaigrette, 102–5
    Shrimp, Andouille, and Corn Gumbo, 88–89
    Shrimp, Peel-and-Eat, 122–24
    Shrimp, Savory BBQ, 49–50
    Stock, Fish, 255
    Stock, Shellfish, 256
    Trout, Pecan-Crusted, with Tomato Bacon Jam, 95–97

French Quarter Dark and Stormy, 235
French toast. See Pain Perdu
The Fried Chicken, 155–57
Fried Green Tomatoes with Buttermilk Dressing, 46–48
Frogs' Legs Sauce Piquant, 120–21
fruit
    crisps and cobblers, 212–17
    in Hattie's Sangria, 234
    Tropical Fruit Salsa, 154
frying technique, 246–48
fundamentals. See basics and fundamentals

G

Gazpacho, 84–85
gin, in Cool as a Cucumber, 239
ginger beer, in French Quarter Dark and Stormy, 235
Good and Evil Chicken Wings, 43–45
graham cracker crust, 228
Gravy, Biscuits and Sausage, 204–5
grits
    Basic, 173–74
    Blue Cheese Grit Cakes, 140–41
    Grits, Watercress, and Brown Butter Balsamic Vinaigrette, Sea Scallops with, 102–5
Gumbo, Shrimp, Andouille, and Corn, 88–89

H

Halibut with Wilted Spinach, Roasted Shiitakes, and Mushroom Nage, 116–19
ham
    hock, in Creole Baked Beans, 165–67
    in Hoppin' John Salad, 190–91
    in Jambalaya, 81–83
    Two Potato Ham Hash, 200–201
Hard Sweet Tea, 242
Hash, Two Potato Ham, 200–201
Hattie's Crawfish/Shrimp Boil, 101
Hattie's Hot Rub
    Cajun Coleslaw, 175
    Caramelized Bacon, 195
    Fried Catfish with Tartar Sauce Two Ways, 92–94
    recipe for, 141

Hattie's Hot Sauce
    Good and Evil Chicken Wings, 43–45
    Spicy Pecans, 30–31
Hattie's Meat Loaf, 150–51
Hattie's Mojito, 237
Hattie's Restaurant
    Café Lena, 19–20
    cookbook, how to use, 25–28
    current owners and staff, 11–14, 20–24
    former owners, 17
    Hattie Moseley Austin, 14–16
    history of, 14–17
    property description, 17–19
Hattie's Sangria, 234
Hominy, Creamy, 160–61
Honey Butter, 34
Hoppin' John Salad, 190–91
horseradish, in Bloody Mary, 240
horseradish, in Mississippi Salsa, 124
Hot Toddy, 241
Hushpuppies with Honey Butter, 32–34

I

ingredients, choosing, 26–27

J

Jam, Tomato Bacon, 97
Jambalaya, 81–83
Jerk Chicken with Tropical Fruit Salsa and Scallion Aioli, 152–54
Jerk Paste, 153

K

kale, in Stone Soup, 86–87
Key Lime Pie, 226–28

L

leeks, in Prosciutto-Wrapped Cod with Vegetables Provençal, 114–15
Lemonade, Back Porch, 238
Lemonade, Fresh, 238
Lemony Dill Tartar Sauce, 94
Lime Mayonnaise, 53
limes, in Key Lime Pie, 226–28
liqueurs
    Cool as a Cucumber, 239
    Hattie's Sangria, 234
    Sazerac, 243

## M

Macaroni and Cheese, 71–73
MacLean, Christel and Colin, 17
mangoes, in Tropical Fruit Salsa, 154
Man-Hattie's, 231
Maple-Cured Pork Tenderloin, Grilled, 130–31
maple syrup, in Candied Sweet Potatoes, 185
Mason Jar Salad, 184
Mayonnaise, Lime, 53
Meat Loaf, Hattie's, 150–51
Mint Julep, 236
Mississippi Salsa, 124
Mojito, Hattie's, 237
Monkfish with Clams and Chorizo, 125–27
Mushrooms, Andouille and Cheddar-Stuffed, 57–58
Mushroom Stock and Nage, 118

## N

Napa Cabbage Slaw, 108
nuts. *See* pecans

## O

oceans, rivers, and ponds. *See* fish and seafood; frogs' legs
Old Bay Seasoning
    Dry Rub, 149
    Hattie's Crawfish/Shrimp Boil, 101
    Hoppin' John Salad, 190–91
    Peel-and-Eat Shrimp, 122–24
Olive Poppers, 42
onions
    Caramelized Onion and Bacon Tart, 35–37
    Caramelized Onions and Bacon, Chicken Livers with, 59–61
    Salmon with Savoy Cabbage, Caramelized Pearl Onions, and Bacon, 109–10
Oysters, Fried, with Napa Cabbage Slaw and Cilantro Chutney, 106–8

## P

Pain Killer, 244
Pain Perdu, 208–9
Pancakes and Waffles, Buttermilk, 206–7
Peach and Blueberry Cobbler, 215–17

pecan(s)
    -Crusted Trout with Tomato Bacon Jam, 95–97
    Pecan Bread Pudding, 220–21
    Pie, 224–25
    Spicy Pecans, 30–31
Peel-and-Eat Shrimp, 122–24
pie(s)
    Key Lime, 226–28
    Pecan, 224–25
    Pie Dough, 258
    shells, prebaking, 258
    Sweet Potato, 218–19
Pigs in a Blanket, Andouille, 38–39
Pimento Cheese, 62–63
Pimento Cheese Sliders, Andouille and, 136–37
pineapple, in Tropical Fruit Salsa, 154
pineapple juice, in Pain Killer, 244
Poppers, Olive, 42
pork
    ground, in Hattie's Meat Loaf, 150–51
    Pork Tenderloin, Grilled Maple-Cured, 130–31
    Ribs Without a Smoker, 147–49
    *See also* bacon; ham; prosciutto; sausage
potatoes
    in Crawfish Boil, 98–101
    in Monkfish with Clams and Chorizo, 125–27
    Smashed Potatoes, 162–64
    in Stone Soup, 86–87
    Two Potato Ham Hash, 200–201
Pot Roast, 132–35
Prosciutto-Wrapped Cod with Vegetables Provençal, 114–15

## R

Red Beans and Rice, 74–75
Relish, Sweet Corn, 53
Ribs Without a Smoker, 147–49
rice
    cooking, 259
    in Crawfish Étouffée, 79–80
    Dirty Rice, 180–81
    in Hoppin' John Salad, 190–91
    in Jambalaya, 81–83
    Red Beans and, 74–75

rum
    Classic Daiquiri, 233
    French Quarter Dark and Stormy, 235
    Hattie's Mojito, 237
    Pain Killer, 244

## S

Saffron, Tomato, and Thyme, Steamed Clams with, 69–70
salad dressings
    Brown Butter Balsamic Vinaigrette, 105
    Brown Butter Lemon Vinaigrette, 113
    Buttermilk Dressing, 48
    Lemon Maple Vinaigrette, 143
    Pecan Blue Cheese Dressing, 45
    Salad Dressing, 184
salads
    Cucumber Salad, 186–87
    Hoppin' John Salad, 190–91
    Mason Jar, 184
    Warm Chicken, Bacon, and Arugula, 142–43
    *See also* coleslaw
Salmon with Savoy Cabbage, Caramelized Pearl Onions, and Bacon, 109–10
salsas
    Mississippi, 124
    Tropical Fruit, 154
sauces
    Bourbon Sauce, 221
    Sauce Piquant, 121
sausage
    Biscuits and Sausage Gravy, 204–5
    in Creole Baked Beans, 165–67
    in Red Beans and Rice, 74–75
    in Savory Corn Bread Pudding, 188–89
    *See also* andouille; chorizo; tasso
Scallion Aioli, 154
scallops
    Seared Sea Scallops with Grits, Watercress, and Brown Butter Balsamic Vinaigrette, 102–5
seafood. *See* fish and seafood
Seasoning Mix, 50
Shiitake Mushrooms, 118

shrimp
    Peel-and-Eat, 122–24
    Savory BBQ, 49–50
    Shrimp, Andouille, and Corn
        Gumbo, 88–89
side dishes, 159–91
    Baked Beans, Creole, 165–67
    Biscuits, 168–69
    Coleslaw, Cajun, 174
    Coleslaw, Cranberry, 178–79
    Collard Greens, 182–83
    Corn and Tasso Spoon Bread,
        170–72
    Corn Bread, 176–77
    Corn Bread Pudding, Savory,
        188–89
    Cucumber Salad, 186–87
    Dirty Rice, 180–81
    Grits, Basic, 173–74
    Hominy, Creamy, 160–61
    Hoppin' John Salad, 190–91
    Salad Dressing (and Mason Jar
        Salad), 184
    Sweet Potatoes, Candied, 185
Simple Syrup, 233
Sliders, Andouille and Pimento Cheese,
    136–37
Smashed Potatoes, 162–64
Smoked Tomato Butter, 140
soups, stews, and bowls, 65–89
    Brisket Chili, 66–68
    Chicken and Dumplings, 76–78
    Clams, Steamed, with Saffron,
        Tomato, and Thyme, 69–70
    Crawfish Étouffée, 79–80
    Gazpacho, 84–85
    Jambalaya, 81–83
    Macaroni and Cheese, 71–73
    Red Beans and Rice, 74–75
    Stone Soup, 86–87
Spicy Pecans, 30–31
Spinach, Wilted, 117–18
Spoon Bread, Corn and Tasso, 170–72
squash, summer, in Prosciutto-

Wrapped Cod with Vegetables
    Provençal, 114–15
starters, nibbles, and noshes, 29–63
    Andouille and Cheddar-Stuffed
        Mushrooms, 57–58
    Andouille Pigs in a Blanket, 38–39
    Caramelized Onion and Bacon Tart,
        35–37
    Cheese Straws and Olive Poppers,
        40–42
    Chicken Livers with Caramelized
        Onions and Bacon, 59–61
    Crab Cakes with Sweet Corn Relish
        and Lime Mayo, 51–53
    Deviled Eggs, 54–56
    Fried Green Tomatoes with
        Buttermilk Dressing, 46–48
    Good and Evil Chicken Wings,
        43–45
    Hushpuppies with Honey Butter,
        32–34
    Pimento Cheese, 62–63
    Savory BBQ Shrimp, 49–50
    Spicy Pecans, 30–31
stews. See soups, stews, and bowls
stock(s)
    Brown Veal, 252–53
    Chicken, 251
    Fish, 255
    making, 249–50
    Mushroom, 118
    Shellfish, 256
    Vegetable, 254
Stone Soup, 86–87
Sweet Corn Relish, 53
sweet potatoes
    Candied, 185
    Sweet Potato Pie, 218–19
    Two Potato Ham Hash, 200–201
Sweet Tea, Hard, 242

T

Tart, Caramelized Onion and Bacon,
    35–37

Tartar Sauce Two Ways, 94
Tasso Spoon Bread, Corn and,
    170–72
tea, iced, in Hard Sweet Tea, 242
tomatoes
    Fried Green, with Buttermilk
        Dressing, 46–48
    in Gazpacho, 84–85
    in Jambalaya, 81–83
    juice, in Bloody Mary, 240
    in Prosciutto-Wrapped Cod with
        Vegetables Provençal, 114–15
    in Sauce Piquant, 121
    Smoked Tomato Butter, 140
    Steamed Clams with Saffron,
        Tomato, and Thyme, 69–70
    Tomato Bacon Jam, 97
topping, rolled oat, 214
Tropical Fruit Salsa, 154
Trout with Tomato Bacon Jam, Pecan-
    Crusted, 95–97
Two Potato Ham Hash, 200–201

V

veal, ground, in Hattie's Meat Loaf,
    150–51
Veal Stock, Brown, 252–53
Vegetables Provençal, Prosciutto-
    Wrapped Cod with, 114–15
Vegetable Stock, 254
vermouth, in Man-Hattie's, 231
vinaigrettes
    Brown Butter Balsamic, 105
    Brown Butter Lemon, 113
    Lemon Maple, 143
vodka, in Back Porch Lemonade, 238
vodka, in Bloody Mary, 240

W

Waffles, Buttermilk Pancakes and,
    206–7
wine, red, in Hattie's Sangria, 234
The World's Best Egg Sandwich, 194–
    95, 194–96